Imagining Culture
New World Narrative and
the Writing of Canada

Many former members of European empires have found it necessary
to overcome the colonial process and assert a "postcolonial" culture.
Imagining Culture applies postcolonial analysis to Canadian literature. Margaret Turner argues that many Canadian texts from the
nineteenth and twentieth centuries are engaged in the creation of a
new discursive space and shows that new world conditions have deci-
sively informed the discourse of the fiction of anglophone Canada.

Turner examines the manner in which a new world culture represents itself, creates its origins, and constructs and understands the
construction of its cultural history. She supports her theory with an
analysis of paradigmatic texts by John Richardson, Frederick Philip
Grove, Sheila Watson, Robert Kroetsch, and Jane Urquhart that
articulate the predicament of the new world writer.

Imagining Culture reveals the haunting of language and imagination that attends the search for origins and belonging and shows
how Canadian writers enact the processes of inhabiting the new
world and imagining its culture.

MARGARET E. TURNER is a specialist in Canadian literature living
in Guelph, Ontario.

P9-BJA-291

Imagining Culture

*New World Narrative
and the Writing
of Canada*

MARGARET E. TURNER

McGill-Queen's University Press
Montreal & Kingston • London • Buffalo

© McGill-Queen's University Press 1995
ISBN 0-7735-1308-6 (cloth)
ISBN 0-7735-1361-2 (paper)

Legal deposit fourth quarter 1995
Bibliothèque nationale du Québec

Printed in Canada on acid-free paper

This book has been published with the help of a grant
from the Canadian Federation for the Humanities, using
funds provided by the Social Sciences and Humanities
Research Council of Canada.

McGill-Queen's University Press is grateful to the Canada
Council for support of its publishing program.

Canadian Cataloguing in Publication Data

Turner, Margaret, 1957–
    Imagining culture : new world narrative and the writing
    of Canada

    Includes bibliographical references and index.
    ISBN 0-7735-1308-6 (bound) –
    ISBN 0-7735-1361-2 (pbk.)

    1. Canadian fiction (English) – History and criticism.
    I. Title.

PS8071.T85 1995   C813.009   C95-900374-6
PR9184.3.T85 1995

Typeset in Sabon 10.5/13
by Caractéra production graphique, Quebec City

Contents

Acknowledgments

This book is concerned with the manner in which a new world culture represents itself, creates its own origins, and constructs and understands its construction of its own cultural history within the ambivalent discursive space of what has been called the middle ground of post-colonialism. I argue that the cognitive and perceptual placement of a new world culture in this distinct discursive universe fundamentally affects the nature of its cultural products and, in particular, its literary texts. In these new world conditions cultural existence is predicated on the ability to negotiate an ambivalent discursive space and to interrogate the new world's way of knowing while showing the processes by which that way of knowing constructs the new world: the new world writer continually remakes the discursive place by rewriting the cultural text.

The body of this study consists of my attempt to articulate this understanding of new world discursive conditions within the context of anglophone Canada and its literature, through a detailed discussion of particular works from the nineteenth and twentieth centuries. I have been, necessarily, selective rather than comprehensive in my choice of texts, choosing several that express with particular clarity the predicament of the new world writer. It remains to be determined if the principles I have formulated here would enrich our understanding of other texts and of our literary and cultural tradition; I believe this is the case, but that work remains to be done.

My personal thanks are due to Jack Healy and Leslie Monkman, who generously read and commented on earlier versions or sections of the manuscript. Jack Healy in particular has been a witness to the many incarnations of this project and an integral influence on my "new world" thinking.

This book was written in large part while I was a Canada Research Fellow in the Department of English at the University of Guelph: I would like to thank the university, the Social Sciences and Humanities Research Council of Canada, and Mutual Life of Canada for their support of the Canada Research Fellowship program.

Imagining Culture

CHAPTER ONE

Introduction:
"Here there be monsters"

The first European encounters with the continental landmass to the west of Europe occurred well before the Renaissance, but not until the late fifteenth and early sixteenth centuries did the European interest in it become sustained and systematic. The first voyages west by Europeans expressed an interest not in finding a new world, which in any case was inconceivable from within a medieval world-view, but in finding a *known* world, the Orient, and an alternative to the voyage around the Cape. Although debate occurred throughout the Middle Ages regarding the proportions of the globe's unsubmerged land and ocean, it was generally agreed that the Island of Earth in the Northern Hemisphere contained as much dry land as could exist and that any as yet unknown islands in either hemisphere would be small and uninhabited (O'Gorman 51–8). Variations on this scheme were argued as interest in the route to the Orient increased, but the consensus remained antithetical to the existence of any large, inhabited landmass. The earliest explorations occurred within this stable framework in which the human being and the physical world were, by and large, fixed and limited entities, each supporting tautologically what was and could be known; faith and cosmography were mutually dependent.

The accidental discovery of the Americas was a disappointment, since the direct route west was effectively blocked, and was incidental to the main European interest and desire with regard to oceanic travel. That initial disappointment was accompanied by other reactions, which found their cause in the fact that an unknown landmass of such magnitude *should not* have existed. The "real" and known world had been precisely delineated from the unknown, or what Juan Promis calls "a circumference of enigmas extending toward the infinite" (1). The adventurers who dared to cross the line were warned by the notation on their maps what to expect: "Here there be monsters" (Promis 1). Those "monsters" turned out not to be the silent void or fantastical beasts anticipated by many (Promis 1) but the radical intellectual and theological shifts necessitated by the new geographical information: the impact of the discovery of a new hemisphere was contemporaneously likened to the most important event since the creation of the world excepting the birth and death of Christ, and later to the invention of the printing press (Slavin 140–1). The newly discovered existence of the Americas refuted the first principles of the universe and of human being: both ancient and Christian thought were at odds with the modern concept that the world was only as limited as the human power required to take possession of it. The effects of this ideological revolution on what suddenly became a question – the nature of human being – would have been profound enough in itself without the added shock that the existence of the indigenous inhabitants of the Americas constituted. The metaphysical accommodation thus required was matched by a physical reorientation as Europe began to face west, a significant act in the impact it had both on the economies of European countries and on their political relations, and which has affected the subsequent histories of both regions in no small way.

The ramifications of the change in thought and belief stemming from the discoveries extend to our own time and to the project I am attempting here: an articulation of the discursive nature of new world cultures and, from that, a reading of a particular new world literature, that of anglophone Canada. The principles of Edward Said's critique of orientalism register in this context: like Said's Orient, what I call here the new world exists as an idea that has a history and a tradition of thought, imagery, and vocabulary that have given it reality and presence. An object of European desire before its existence was known, "America" is an idea constructed by the European imagination. The nature and the cultural history of the new world have been determined by the expectations imposed upon it, its "discovery" constituted by the intellectual and imaginative preparation for it, which in turn constructed its social reality: the meaning of the new lands was necessarily the meaning that corresponded to them within the new picture of the world that they themselves promoted (O'Gorman 130). This intellectual or figurative invention persisted even when the Americas became known, and determined the shape and nature of what they could become. Their discovery changed the idea of history: the Americas existed as both a fixed physical entity and a spiritual entity capable of realizing itself within the sphere of historical being (O'Gorman 140).

In the context of this study, then, "new world" refers to the Americas that Europeans invented for themselves and colonized, not the landmasses that were the home of coherent and permanent native cultures. My book addresses these European processes without discounting the fact that the Americas were not new in any sense to the people who had lived in them for centuries; that in making their claim of newness, Europeans dispossessed natives and appropriated both land and language; that since that initial dispossession indigenous peoples have been systematically excluded from history, culture, and power in their own place; that this exclusion has in various forms effected a brutal suppression of the native voice. This positioning not only makes the problematic terminology associated with the topic comprehensible and, in a particular way, accurate – from a strictly European point of view, Europeans did "discover" their own "new" world – but makes visible and, perhaps, emphasizes the processes of the construction of the European position with regard to the native. It does not excuse or justify the acts, based on those processes, that have had such a profound and devastating impact on native culture and history in the Americas. Europeans made their own new world, for themselves. In many ways they invented it before they knew it: in so doing their possession of it was guaranteed. That Europeans felt it necessary to eradicate native structures and values in order to establish their own and to deny the idea of literate and historically conscious native cultures is both tragic and ironic and speaks the whole discourse of power enacted in colonialism.

What Europeans came to know as their new world was not the reality that its natives inhabited. In *Marvellous Possessions* Stephen Greenblatt argues that wonder is "the central figure in the initial European response to the New World" (14). He finds the sense of wonder, which he understands as a deeply internal experience occurring "at the vital, emotional center of the witness" (16), integral to the early European discursive responses to the new world. Although wonder was at the time already part of the discourses of philosophy and art, Greenblatt argues that the frequency and intensity of the appeal to wonder following the age of the discoveries helped to provoke its conceptualization. Most useful in Greenblatt's study of the nature and function of discursive practices in the new world is his linkage of processes of conceptualization with representational practices. Greenblatt describes the experience of wonder as seeming "to resist recuperation, containment, ideological incorporation" and existing "apart from everything that gives coherence to [the] universe" (17). I will argue here that this resistance to containment and ideological incorporation is not limited to the initial expressions of new world experience but has continued to inform the discourse of fiction in English-speaking Canada. Greenblatt's sense of wonder or of radical displacement that signals the loss of a coherent universe accounts, I believe, for the power and resonance of some of the most interesting writing coming out of this new world culture.

Greenblatt juxtaposes the European representation of non-Europeans with the European act of taking possession of the new world: discursive technology is implicated in both procedures. In his study of the European encounter with the new world Tzvetan Todorov argues that a difference in discursive technology was decisive in determining the nature of the Spanish presence in middle America and the subsequent conquest of the continent. Although Greenblatt takes issue with both Todorov's interpretation of the American cultures' representational technology and his linkage of writing with power (11ff.), both arguments situate us precisely in a particular context – the function of discourse in the construction of the new world. Any understanding of the new world's subsequent cultural history and production rests on that point. Todorov goes so far as to argue that the events of discovery and conquest have determined not only the history and perceptual placement of the Americas but the nature of human being in the modern period (5). In Europe's initial complete ignorance of the new world, what should have been an apprehension of difference was instead an apprehension of absence: the perceived absences of language, law, and religion led Europe to posit a total lack of indigenous spiritual and material culture in the new world (Todorov 35). Todorov goes on to develop the concept of alterity, which is the basis of *The Conquest of America*,[1] but his comments about native speech and the European perception of it deserve particular emphasis. The discursive basis of the new world makes understandable the erasure of the coherent culture of natives who are judged for a lack of speech – European speech: on his first voyage Columbus took six natives back to Europe so they could be taught "to speak" (Todorov 30). The appropriation of native space, erasure of native language, and annihilation of native life thus become, according to a particular logic, more justifiable: the natives have less claim to their own territory and right of self-determination since they cannot express it in a way of speaking that is understood or even categorized as human language by Europeans. This raises the recurrent question of the nature of the new world human in the context of slaughter, eradication, and marginalization.

The ability of Europe to create the new world was dependent on the European inability to perceive or conceptualize the Americas or, to use Greenblatt's terms, on the Americas' continued resistance to recuperation, containment, and ideological incorporation by Europe. Even after exploration began in earnest, what Greenblatt refers to as a "cracking apart of contextual understanding" (19) persisted, not because of a simple inability to communicate but because of a refusal to acknowledge the two completely separate and incompatible discursive universes the native and European cultures inhabited. Throughout his voyages of exploration Columbus insisted that natives provided the information that influenced his subsequent actions – information that happened to correspond directly to his desire for reports of wealth and the proximity of great cities, for example – and this despite the fact that he admitted that he and his men could not understand the native languages except by conjecture (Todorov 29–33; Greenblatt 13–14). Todorov argues that this lack of attention to the other's language is crucial in understanding how Europeans conquered the new world: the European failure fully to recognize and comprehend the natives' otherness, which registered linguistically as well as in other ways, led to the transformation of native Americans from subject to object (49) and subsequently to the determining events of the Conquest, which were enabled by the native loss of control over communication (61–2).

Greenblatt's interpretation of Columbus's act of possession is this: "For Columbus taking possession is principally the performance of a set of linguistic acts: declaring, witnessing, recording," performed for a world elsewhere (56–7). He argues further that the extreme formalism of Columbus's linguistic acts – the making of the required declarations – "tries to make the new lands uninhabited ... by emptying out the category of the other. The other exists only as an empty sign, a cipher. Hence there can be no contradiction to the proclamation [of possession] from anyone on the islands themselves, because only linguistic competence, the ability to understand and to speak, would enable one to fill in the sign ... When the moment arrived to contradict the proclamation, those [Europeans] who could contradict it were absent, and all subsequent claims will be forever belated and thus invalid" (60). This reading of Columbus's actions, it seems to me, bears some relation to what Gayatri Chakravorty Spivak calls "othering": the projection of one's own codes on to what is perceived to be the vacant – or emptied – territory of the other.[2] Despite the differences in the ways Todorov, Greenblatt, and Spivak regard the European attitude and actions toward the natives of the new world, the conclusion is the same: in not allowing the possibility of the natives' otherness, in "emptying out" the category of the other, in transforming and then recuperating the other by means of European codes of cultural recognition, the Europeans profoundly negated the existence of the native population long before the impact of the first musket or microbe. Europeans performed acts of possession to place the new world firmly within the known universe of territorial claim and legal record: "Writing here fixes a set of public linguistic acts, gives them official standing, makes them 'historical' events" (Greenblatt 58). I will return later to the problematic status of history as it pertains to the discursive nature of the new world, but the European necessity for a written record in this context must be registered. Where previously "Here there be monsters" had signified the dangerous unknown, the new notations of San Salvador, Isla de Santa Maria de Concepcion, Fernandina, Isabella, and Isla Juana[3] asserted human (sic) presence and the resolution of enigma.

A discursive strategy thus creates a new world. That strategy is dependent on the provenance of European systems of perception, conceptualization, and representation. The new world thus created does not reflect the physical or cultural actuality in which it occurs; the European system in the new world could only consolidate its own intellectual processes, with the result that its hegemony was not seriously questioned by Europeans themselves. These processes and their results constitute in part the procedure by which European imperialism has shaped and determined the new world's cultural history and, more important here, has determined what can be known of new world cultures and by what means. The results of those processes have a bearing on the transplanted European society that followed and on that society's attempts to deal not only with the new space but, as Alan Lawson puts it, with the "inherent awareness of both 'there' and 'here'" (quoted in Slemon "Resistance" 38) – the primary predicament of the new world writer, which I will be discussing in detail in the following chapters.

The European discovery of the new world, then, is most important not in geographical terms as a purposeful act of scientific significance, which it was not, but as an act of perception and imagination. O'Gorman argues this essential distinction: the new world was imagined – invented by the European imagination – rather than found. It follows, then, that the vocabulary that has shaped the knowledge and attitude about the European presence in the Americas is profoundly *wrong*:[4] "America" was not and could not have been "discovered" by Europeans until its existence was known. In O'Gorman's words: "the fault that lies at the root of the entire history of the idea of the discovery of America consists in assuming that the lump of cosmic matter which we now know as the American continent has always been that, when actually it only became that when such a meaning was given to it, and will cease to be that when, by virtue of some change in the current world concept, that meaning will no longer be assigned to it" (42). Like Columbus's, our "knowing" has been a contradiction of fact.

Columbus decided before leaving Europe on his first voyage west that any land he encountered would have to be the Asian continent: his conviction that reaching the Orient on a voyage west was inevitable secured him the support he required. His first image of the Americas, which became widely propagated, was determined before sailing and based on information and preconceptualizations that originated before the voyage: in that sense new world experience began on European ground (Malkiel 583). When the events of the voyages did not conform to his expectations, it was not so much the idea of the new passage to the East that was compromised but his own credibility: during the second voyage Columbus forced his crew, under threat, to swear that the land they had encountered, actually Cuba, was too large to be an island and thus had to be

Asia (O'Gorman 89–90) – another action in which witness and declaration create reality, and geographical and experiential evidence do not register as contradiction. Columbus never admitted that the land he encountered in his four voyages was not the Orient: in spite of conflicting evidence and the necessity to adjust his data accordingly, he continued to maintain that this territory was part of the one known world. What is more interesting than Columbus's logical contortions is that his version of the "Indies," or significant parts of it, was largely accepted: he not only denied the existence of what was actually there but constructed his own reality and the European attitudes and language about the Americas and their natives that would be current for centuries. It is both ironic and fitting that Amerigo Vespucci's name, rather than Columbus's, became America's; only gradually and *in spite of* Columbus's intentions did the evidence of his voyages, particularly his fourth, in conjunction with Vespucci's first, establish that the Americas were not the Malay peninsula, which could be sailed around to reach China, but an unknown continent stretching from north to south through the Atlantic.

In a very real sense the naming of America signals its invention – its inclusion in European discourse was according to its perceptual placement by Europe. Recognition of the discursive extent of its invention makes the processes of cultural and historical construction visible and provokes an interrogation of the manner in which such intellectual processes both make conceptual space for new understandings and create the concept that fills that space. To point up the way in which an entire hemisphere and its cultural products have been constructed is to point up the discursive nature of the new world.

The assumption that communication could occur between groups and across languages on the one hand, and the early accruing of power to translators and interpreters on the other (Todorov 98–123; Greenblatt 139–51), draws attention to both the contradiction and the centrality of language in the possession of the Americas as well as to the ambiguous authority attached to articulation and inscription. The first new world writing by Europeans was not determined by the new world but by the pressure of maintaining the imperial continuum and the necessity of constructing a point of view from which new world experience would be coherent and intelligible. It has been necessary to rehearse the European actions and reactions at the time of the discoveries in order to situate the central premise of this study; I would like to turn now to a consideration of the ways in which the new world began to occupy its discursive space.

The discourse of the new world begins with the discourse of discovery and includes the early rumours and unconfirmed reports of rich fishing grounds and accidental Norse encounters with land in the west, as well as the documentation of the explorations of the late fifteenth and early sixteenth centuries.[5] With increasing contact and exploration there is an increase of both number and kind of texts: Columbus's letters and correspondence, the journals, maps, and books of other explorers, the commentaries of Europeans travelling in the Americas, the descriptive catalogues of the physical and social nature of the Americas. The problematic nature of language in the new world – how to communicate with the natives in other than mute signs or material exchange, how even to categorize fauna or describe landforms – is immediately apparent and is recorded disparately in accounts of misunderstandings and failed communication between Europeans and natives, in the assumption of what Greenblatt calls cultural transparency, in Gonzalo Fernandez de Oviedo's and José d'Acosta's accounts of inaccurate nomenclature (Gerbi 28). The early European new world texts also exhibit the European anxiety of definition in attempts to draw comparisons between old and new worlds, which eventually engaged two centuries of old and new world intellectuals – scientists, historians, theologians, poets, philosophers – in a debate on the comparative, quantitative value of Europe and the Americas.[6]

Inaccurate nomenclature has not been unique to the European experience in the Americas,[7] but in this context it emphasizes a more general European inability to perceive and conceptualize the new world and defines the discursive gap into which, from a European viewpoint, the new world fell. The use of the wrong names on dissimilar phenomena is one indication of the paucity of European language that could be meaningfully applied to the new world. Another is the accounts of Europeans unable to articulate their new world experiences. One such example is from Hernando Cortés. After finding it impossible to describe the palace of Montezuma in a letter to Charles V, Cortés is brought to silence by a native market: "Finally, besides those things which I have already mentioned, they sell in the market everything else to be found in this land, but they are so many and so varied that because of their great number and because I cannot remember many of them nor do I know what they are called I shall not mention them" (quoted in Franklin 3). Cortés's first equation of number and variety of objects is perhaps not unexpected, but his subsequent equation of those factors with his own faulty memory, which is *then* linked with his lack of native vocabulary, betrays a significant pattern in European thinking. Cortés admits that a native vocabulary exists and that he does not know it, as well as that his own conceptual powers are insufficient to the task of likening the things in the market to old world objects, or even describing them in their own terms. He also admits his anxiety in these conditions. With or without his rationalization, the market remains – silently – inside Greenblatt's aura of wonder and outside of European conceptualization or representation. Another example comes from Bernal Diaz's description of the Aztec capital, in which he resorts to the language of medieval romance, *Amadis of Gaul*, before he too falls silent: "Gazing on such wonderful sights, we did not know what to say, or whether what appeared before us was real" (quoted in Greenblatt 133). (We will hear a close echo of this difficulty in assessing reality later, from John Richardson.) The European difficulty in seeing and speaking needed to be resolved; Greenblatt's suggestion that Europeans used violent action to do so (133–5) would go some way in explaining the brutality of European acts of appropriation in the new world.

The complex relationship of vision and articulation sketched here, however, is not confined to the experience of Europeans in the Americas. Helen Tiffin describes it as the "double vision characteristic of all post-colonial peoples – the tension between imported (and imposed) language and the realities of the surrounding environment," and reiterates it as one of the twin bases of comparative post-colonial literary criticism ("Methodology" 29). I will return to the problematic "all post-colonial peoples" a little later, but for the moment I would like to look briefly at the context she invokes, post-colonial literary criticism, and at how post-colonialism is generally understood.[8] Tiffin describes post-colonial cultures as "inevitably hybridized, involving a dialectical relationship between European ontology and epistemology and the impulse to create or recreate an independent local identity" ("Counter-Discourse" 17). That impulse is motivated by the historical construction or reconstruction of identities and places of colonized peoples by the cognitive codes of Europe and by the existence of the European historical and fictional record, in which the figures of the language itself – tropes, forms, themes, myths – operate not as cultural expression but as cultural control ("Recuperative" 27–8); it issues into the processes of artistic and literary decolonization that Tiffin calls counter-discourse, which have involved "a radical dis/mantling of European codes and a post-colonial subversion and appropriation of the dominant European discourses" ("Counter-Discourse" 17). The counter-discursive strategies employed by post-colonial texts vary; Linda Hutcheon has examined in some detail the function of irony in post-colonial texts, Stephen Slemon of magic realism and allegory. Tiffin sees counter-discourse using not only tropes but entire reading strategies; she explores in some detail Wilson Harris's concept of infinite rehearsal, whereby the repeated rereading of a particular cultural text interrogates and revises imposed cognitive orders while simultaneously interrogating its own biases ("Recuperative," "Counter-Discourse"). With others, she also argues that rather than closure – the privileging of one set of cognitive codes over others in the establishment of national or regional traditions – a reopening or refusal of finality is characteristic of post-colonial literatures.

Just as reality is not the same for Europeans and natives, neither is it the same for "all post-colonial peoples." Tiffin delineates patterns of colonialism that have had particular results; one such is the ambiguous position of white settler societies, inhabiting what Slemon calls colonialism's middle ground ("Resistance" 34). As Tiffin points out, the white population, transplanted or transported to decimate or annihilate an indigenous population, brings with it a culture and language evolved elsewhere ("Methodology" 30); although still colonized itself by Europe, it acts in turn as the colonizer of the indigenous population ("Counter-Discourse" 20). Hutcheon discusses in some detail just how the definition of post-coloniality can be applied to the particular middle ground that Canadian culture occupies. She argues the impossibility of equating Canada with third world post-colonial cultures and draws attention to the multiracial nature of Canadian society as well as to the doubled colonial focus that results from its experience of American imperialism ("Downspout" 155–60; *Splitting* 74–9). For our purposes Hutcheon's argument is most useful in describing Canada's (and, by implication, other originally white settler societies') differentiation from third world post-colonial cultures, a differentiation that Slemon takes up in his exploration of the "neither/nor territory of white settler-colonial writing which Alan Lawson has called the 'Second World.'"[9] Slemon argues that the second world has been foreclosed from post-colonial literary representations because it is not sufficiently pure in its anti-colonialism, it does not offer up an experiential grounding in a common third world aesthetics, and its modalities of post-coloniality are too ambivalent, too occasional, and too uncommon. He contends that the ambivalence of literary resistance itself defines the condition of the second world: the inherent awareness of both there *and* here, the lack of a stable self/other, here/there binary division, which has been thought to be characteristic of post-colonial experience, constitutes the second world's profound ambivalence. Thus in Slemon's argument the mediated, conditional, and radically compromised literatures of this second world fulfil the limits and conditions of post-colonial forms of literary resistance.

I find Slemon's theorizing of the second world useful not only for its emphasis on the seemingly contradictory, neither/nor aspects of the second world's existence that produce its condition of radical ambivalence, but for its opening of a space for the creation of yet a third discursive universe, existing simultaneously *between* and *in relation to* European certainties and the circumference of enigmas that the Western Hemisphere once represented. If "here there be monsters" at all, they have been the expectations that second world literatures would conform to first (or more recently even third) world literary models (as Tiffin and others point out, the task of persuading critics to acknowledge that the first world is not the only model is arduous enough). Those expectations, as we well know, determined the accounts of Canada's literary history that circulated throughout the last century, endured until regrettably recently in our own, and, by ignoring the political and historical context, caused powerful and even radically original works of Canadian writers to be read as derivative and subsidiary. Banishing those monsters requires a restoration of context, a rereading of texts, a reinterpretation of codes, an opening of textual containment. It follows that this shift in perspective, this recognition of the separate discursive universe of the second world, is actually a recognition that the question these cultural products address is not ways of *being* in the new world, but ways of *knowing*. This is consistent with post-colonial theorizing: Tiffin holds that ways of knowing are crucial to the investigation and interrogation of the processes whereby post-colonial realities are constructed by the imperial perspective ("Recuperative" 31). Understanding Canadian literature as a discourse that interrogates our ways of knowing would result in a radical rereading of texts and recasting of literary history.

Earlier I pointed to the problematic status of the notion of history in the new world. I would like to discuss that point now in conjunction with this orientation towards ways of knowing. The work of Michel Foucault, Hayden White, and others has shown that historical writing is a complex discourse, relying as it does on rhetorical structures and techniques of narrative and mediated by culture and ideology. We know as well that a very strong temptation towards history is operative in new cultures, a temptation Homi Bhabha describes as "the familiar quest for an origin that will authorize a beginning." Although I take his point, I do not agree with the totalizing inevitability he suggests in the same argument, that "the demand for a literary tradition, a history, is put in exactly the same historicist and realist terms" as the imperial culture (quoted in Tiffin "Counter-Discourse" 21).

Colin Partridge makes a distinctly different argument. In his interpretation of the formation of new cultures he suggests a common series of acts that serve to clarify the human relationship with the new environment. One of these is making myth and metaphor, which he describes as the home-made legend through which later inhabitants will view the place's origin and development: as factual history is succeeded in general consciousness by poetic or mythic history, the new culture comes to shape people's perceptions of the past (18). He argues further that in the making of new cultures these distinctive processes or experiences "contribute to modes of perception that have no counterpart in older societies. The new literatures dramatize these processes because, generally, artists in new cultures remain aware of the formative cultural forces" (30). Partridge makes what is for my argument the crucial link between modes of perception and the construction of cultural origins or, as Bhabha puts it, the origin that will authorize a beginning. Partridge's formulation of new cultures includes, then, the unique processes by which they simultaneously construct *and understand their construction of* their own cultural history – in other words, their ways of knowing. This perceptual and cognitive placement is precisely what determines my choice of the writers and texts that I discuss in the following chapters: although the five writers studied here make the new culture's demand for a literary tradition and a history, they do so on the terms of the new culture rather than of the old. Rather than replicating imperial cognitive processes, as Bhabha argues, they both exhibit and act upon their perceptual and cognitive placement in the new world: they interrogate the new world's way of knowing as they show the processes by which that way of knowing constructs the new world.

The new world's perceptual and cognitive placement results in particular characteristics of expression: continuing and recurring silences, sudden gaps in which questions can or cannot be asked, the sense that literature written in and out of this context *means* in a way that is not so for the writing of cultures that did not come into existence in this way. George Grant's understanding of the need to create a cultural origin underlines Partridge's argument: "[The majestic continent] could not be ours in the old way because the making of it ours did not go back before the beginning of conscious memory. The roots of some communities in eastern North America go back far in continuous love for their place, but none of us can be called autochthonous, because in all there is some consciousness of making the land our own" (17). The gap between the new world's physical existence and its discursive invention ensures that its European inhabitants are under the extreme pressure of Tiffin's double vision or, in another formulation, what Peter Hulme calls colonialist discourse. As Hulme describes it, colonialist discourse speaks the existence of two worlds: "a world of civility ..., of legal and governmental institutions, of contracts and guarantees, where words are embedded in solid and stable discursive practices; and an alien and hostile world where words, like actions, are improvised in a savage void, having no resonance beyond their immediate effect. Colonialist discourse has no memory – which is only another way of saying it has no narrative – until it provokes the occurrence that it will never forget" (156). We have returned to Greenblatt's separate discursive universes and the argument I made earlier, that

the new world's resistance to containment and ideological incorporation is not limited to the initial expressions of new world experience but has continued to inform the discourse of fiction of
English-speaking Canada.

The remainder of this study articulates this understanding of
anglophone Canadian literature by the close analysis of several
nineteenth- and twentieth-century texts with a view to determining
how and to what extent the middle ground, neither/nor, second
world conditions of anglophone Canada register within them.[10] As
I hope is apparent by now, I am particularly interested in how this
culture represents itself, how it creates its origin, how it constructs
and understands its construction of its own cultural history. I hope,
in my readings of particular texts, to show that this culture's
existence is predicated on its knowledge of how discourse works –
both its own cognitive codes and those of Europe – and, thus, its
ability to negotiate its own inevitable hybridization. I will argue
that Harris's notion of infinite rehearsal is particularly apt in anglophone Canada: that the simultaneous construction and representation of the culture results in a continual remaking of the discursive
place, or recreation of cultural space in which, as Paul Carter puts
it, places might eventually be found (32).

The stutters and pauses in the occupation of that discursive space
are audible, as are the voices that articulate with great clarity the
predicament of the new world writer. There are several such voices;
the five I have chosen, ranging from the early nineteenth to the late
twentieth centuries, demonstrate this clarity of voice and demonstrate as well that what is essentially the same activity, predicated
on similar conditions – the remaking of the discursive place – has
occurred repeatedly over time. To recall Bhabha's words, the writers
and texts discussed here are preoccupied with finding an origin that
will authorize a beginning; in different generations they return to
the same ground to reread and rewrite the cultural text. The nature
of the activity does not change; what the temporal placement does
vary is the range of earlier texts to work against, the available
theoretical apparatus, and the writers' level of anxiety. The writers
I discuss here – John Richardson, Frederick Philip Grove, Sheila
Watson, Robert Kroetsch, and Jane Urquhart – occupy the ambivalent space of the second world and are profoundly aware of both
here and there as well as of the necessity to negotiate that hybridization. These writers exhibit and act upon their perceptual and

cognitive placement; their texts interrogate the new world's way of knowing as they show that way of knowing in the process of constructing the new world.

The writing of John Richardson reveals the trauma of his new world experience. There is nothing solid or stable about the discursive practices available to him: he is in Hulme's alien and hostile world, in which words and actions are continually improvised and have no resonance. Richardson cannot make his voice heard over the musket-fire, shouted orders, and war whoops in *Wacousta*; in neither the British military, the colonial administration, nor the British North American public can he find recognition of himself as author or individual. His birth in British North America and his participation in the War of 1812 as a teenager neither save him from the cultural dislocation of the immigrant nor consolidate his sense of cultural belonging; although his training and class-consciousness are firmly British, it is clear from his writing that the cultural accommodation required by the new world both preoccupies and haunts him.[11] His inhabitation of the new world is figured in military campaigns that result in ambivalent encounters with natives who are identified with the geographical wilderness and represent what has to be removed, or at least made invisible, for European life to be possible in the new world. The ambivalence of those encounters is caused for Richardson by his knowledge that building forts and pushing natives back into the forest will not allow Europeans to inhabit the country in any intellectual or imaginative sense, and expressed in his critical questioning of the old world's definitions of civilization and savagery. *Wacousta*, the text I discuss in detail here, is his first new world novel and an extremely revealing paradigm of cultural contact between Europeans and North American natives. Richardson is on both sides: caught between two modes of thinking and being, he cannot find a space for himself. His literary documentation of that condition shows that his attempt was both unlikely and impossible.

Frederick Philip Grove is similarly obsessed with cultural accommodation. He too finds himself between worlds as an immigrant whose first language is not the language of the country and, for a time, as a pioneer in the Canadian west. Grove's lived biography makes ironic the statements about the personal and cultural costs of the immigration process; that irony opens up a terrain that extends beyond his particular circumstances in Manitoba. In his chronicle of new world experience, *A Search for America*, he provides his definition of the place he landed in relation to the place he left and of which he cannot speak. Grove lives the rhetorical construction of the new world in a singular and unique way; not surprisingly, his writing gives access to this area of concern in a particularly pointed manner, one that goes beyond the personal experiences of an individual and makes visible the theoretical implications of new world experience in Canadian literature. Grove encounters difficulties in living and writing similar in kind to those of earlier writers like Richardson, but his choices are different. Richardson is caught between the European frame, which is still at least partially available to him, and the new world's void of silence and absence. In contrast, Grove has the non-choice of the lost European frame and the newly articulated Canadian one. He is moving into a structure that is only incidentally the Canadian prairie but essentially the new world's distinct discursive universe. This gives resonance to his search for America and its Abe Lincolns. Literally, of course, he can find neither in Canada; his search, however, is not literal. He must create discursive practices that are solid and stable enough to allow his new world life. Grove's life and work are a precise enactment of the processes and conditions of occupying the discursive space of the new world.

Sheila Watson's work continues to be read as a turning-point in anglophone Canadian writing: *The Double Hook*, published in 1959, is the first text to pose Canadian cultural formation directly as a problem of and in language. Watson is very early to recognize and articulate the textual nature of the new world; her explicit linking of textual and cultural construction made possible particular work in Canadian literary and cultural theory. The uniqueness of *The Double Hook* has been recognized by both writers and critics; Watson's deliberate and self-conscious exploration of the discursive nature of Canada and Canadian literature exhibits a sophisticated theoretical awareness of the manner in which the relationship between literary discourse and cultural formation moves both ways. In the novel she creates a new world out of the discourses of native and classical myth, modern literature, the Bible, and Roman Catholic liturgy; metaphorically, the novel represents the new world process of assembling varied cultural elements into a new whole. The explosive juxtaposition of such radically different elements creates in her novel, as in Canadian society, a necessarily uneasy resolution.

Watson is both playful and deadly serious: the world can be spoken into existence by will and whim, or can unravel into absence and silence; the ways in which human life has been made possible in the new world are never stable or secure, and cannot be taken for granted. The strangeness of the world in the novel is both recognizable and disorienting; as Watson sounds resonances that evoke and deny the possibility of sure knowing and being in this place, she expresses the tentative nature of the new world's discursive construction. The 1992 publication of *Deep Hollow Creek*, written before *The Double Hook*, emphasizes much of what is important about *The Double Hook*. Watson's decision not to publish *Deep Hollow Creek* when it was written but to proceed with the second novel, in which the world is much less fixed, the characters more clearly figures, and the elements that could be interpreted autobiographically removed, points even more clearly to the discursive possession of place through imagination and metaphor enacted by *The Double Hook*.

Watson's demonstration of the processes of discursive and cultural construction has facilitated access to theoretical issues that have been engaged subsequently by Canadian writers and critics. One of those is Robert Kroetsch. Watson reclaims an absurd and insubstantial landscape through metaphor; Kroetsch looks again at landscape and *places* the new discursive structure – in his terms, the fiction makes us real. In much of his fiction Kroetsch takes a playful and ironic look at the discursive nature of Canada; in a now-famous essay published in 1974 he discusses the Canadian predicament of borrowed language and offers an early conceptualization of culture, colonialism, and the particular new world condition of Canada. The novel I discuss in detail here, *Gone Indian*, makes the discursive construction of self and place the basis of the novel's form as well as of its narrative line. The resulting treatment of character, plot, and closure echo the openness, possibility, and promise that, for Kroetsch, inform the conditions of the new world. We are some distance here from the forest that threatens to swallow Richardson or the nothingness on the other side of Watson's hill: in *Gone Indian* Jeremy desires rather than dreads the possibilities that disappearing into the landscape will allow. The novel demonstrates the position Kroetsch takes in his critical work, that a cultural place exists only in its discursive reality. Much of Kroetsch's subsequent work has been critically located within the terms of the postmodern, with his interest in language and resistance to meta-narratives. This reading is accurate enough, but I think those characteristics of his work are first expressed through his early interest in the new world conditions he articulates in *Gone Indian*.

Jane Urquhart's *The Whirlpool* brings us full circle, back to John Richardson's historical terrain and the War of 1812 and to questions of how and what we know. Of all the novels discussed here, *The Whirlpool* interrogates most explicitly the relationships between discursive systems and the cultural constructions in which they occur: how the new world perceives, conceptualizes, and represents itself. In *The Whirlpool* all discourses are inadequate and problematic: the novel's poet, who writes mostly of pine trees, is silenced by his inability to differentiate between being and knowing; the novel's historian, a Canadian officer in the British military and a Canadian nationalist, is determined to correct the British and American records of the War of 1812 with the "true" Canadian one. Other discursive possibilities are represented by an autistic child, one woman whose reality is increasingly constituted within her journal and her reading of Robert Browning, and another who wants to reconstruct the stories of the floaters turned up by the Niagara River. Urquhart uses real poles of new world experience to structure her text: her attention to physical and territorial boundaries – the Niagara frontier – reflects the space/place physical/conceptual negotiation that runs through all these novels. She also draws directly on other new world texts: a record from a nineteenth-century undertaking establishment of bodies recovered from the Niagara River, and an early twentieth-century autobiographical work set at the Niagara whirlpool.[12] Urquhart provokes serious and poetic resonances not unlike Watson's with the defining metaphor of her novel, the whirlpool. She also makes sure we understand that the cultural text must be continually reread and rewritten to retain meaning.

We remain haunted by the monsters of the new world, although they are of a different order from those feared by the explorers of the European Renaissance. The loss of a coherent universe attendant upon the transferral of a European population to the new world ensures that Northrop Frye's well-known question is the right one: the answers that writers in anglophone Canada have formulated to "Where is here?" have depended upon their awareness that how we exist and how we know are essentially linked to how a culture represents itelf. The attempt to occupy a distinct and separate discursive space between certainty and enigma is both agonizing and exhilarating. Silence is a real possibility for a culture created in this way, as are an infinite number of new beginnings.

CHAPTER TWO

John Richardson: "A World of Our Own Creation"

John Richardson inhabits an incoherent universe; his attempts to make himself and his place visible and intelligible preoccupy his writing career from the publication of *Tecumseh* in 1828 to his nightmare novels of the early 1850s, *The Monk Knight of St. John* and *Westbrook, the Outlaw; or, The Avenging Wolf*. Richardson's fiction belongs in the category of new world discourse; it is informed by those conditions of displacement and characterized by anxiety and distortion. His writings as a journalist and historian are similarly caused by his need both to see himself in the new world and to have his imaginative construction of that world, along with his presence there, acknowledged. Of all his work, Richardson's first new world novel, *Wacousta or, The Prophecy; A Tale of the Canadas*, published in 1832, shows most clearly both the causes and effects of the discursive construction of the new world. The world that he attempts to transform from unshaped wilderness to stable and civil colonial space resists his efforts: it remains mined with anxiety, threatened by annihilation, guaranteed by treachery, horror, and death.

Wacousta is revealing from a number of points of view: as a document of life in British North America at the time of the Ponteac[1] Conspiracy, as a record of military and political strategy in the period, as an example of early Canadian fiction, as an early nineteenth-century study of genre and influence. It is most revealing, however, as an imaginative construction of the new world. Richardson does not simply record a geographical and historical setting for his treatment of the Ponteac Conspiracy. He creates the world he inhabits in British North America: "It is in solitude, our thoughts, taking their colouring from our feelings, invest themselves with the power of multiplying ideal beauty, until we become in a measure tenants of a world of our own creation, from which we never descend, without loathing and disgust, into the dull and matter-of-fact routine of actual existence. Hence the misery of the imaginative man! – hence his little sympathy with the mass, who, tame and soulless, look upon life and the things of life, not through the refining medium of ideality, but through the grossly magnifying optics of mere sense and materialism" (100). The refining medium of ideality does not precisely fail Richardson in *Wacousta*, but it does refract his line of vision so that he sees only the extremes of sublime landscape and heightened feelings, or a chaos of darkness, terror, and death. What is grossly magnified for him are the senses: while his eyes strain to penetrate the wall of forest surrounding Detroit, his acute hearing detects not only the shrieks and war whoops of attacking Indians but the barely audible rustle of leaves, whispered messages, and muffled oars that may signal either massacre or deliverance. Richardson also feels his own blood grow cold when a mysterious intruder slips into the fort, when an apparent ghost rises from a canoe on Lake Huron, when Wacousta, standing on the "Bloody Bridge," fulfils Ellen Halloway's curse on the De Haldimar family. The threat of impending horrific annihilation permeates Richardson's text; the new world, which he both creates and inhabits, is characterized by chaos and nightmare.

The opening chapter of *Wacousta* clearly signals Richardson's preoccupations:

As we are about to introduce our readers to scenes with which the European is little familiarised, some few cursory remarks, illustrative of the general features of the country into which we have shifted our labours, may not be deemed misplaced at the opening of this volume.

Without entering into minute geographical detail, it may be necessary merely to point out the outline of such portions of the vast continent of America as still acknowledge allegiance to the English crown, in order that the reader, understanding the localities, may enter with deeper interest into the incidents of a tale connected with a ground hitherto untouched by the wand of the modern novelist. (3)

Richardson proceeds by drawing not only the outline but many of the details of the North American continent centred on the Great

Lakes. He begins by moving in from the Atlantic fog up the St Lawrence, but abruptly reconsiders and restarts his "panoramic picture" (4) with the western extremity of settlement at Michilli-mackinac, at the head of Lakes Michigan and Huron. He traces the lake and river system back down to the St Lawrence, describing the sequence of scenes in terms of their majesty, splendour, and magnificence; he focuses on the Great Lakes system since it is a natural barrier between British and American territory in the new world and Richardson understands the world in terms of political, military, and personal allegiance. As he proceeds through the water-way he also draws our attention to the sites of conflict in the 1812 war in which he participated: after its geographical placement, the new world attains its meaning as it is informed by human action in circumstances that are definitive for Richardson's personality and character. It is crucial for Richardson that his readers be able to *see* the new world: clearly he feels he has to show how it appears on a map and to eyes accustomed to European landscapes before he can begin the action of his novel. The geographical and pictorial definitions, however, cannot be separated from the historical and personal events that give that geography and landscape its meaning for Richardson.

The visual sense is important, too, to show what *cannot* be seen of the new world. On the eastern edge of the new world, facing Europe, the view deteriorates rapidly: "From this point the St. Lawrence increases in expanse, until, at length, ... she finally merges in the gulf, from the centre of which the shores on either hand are often invisible to the naked eye; and in this manner is it imperceptibly lost in that misty ocean, so dangerous to mariners from its deceptive and almost perpetual fogs" (5). The new world itself disappears in these conditions; similarly, access to Europe is invisible, if it even exists. At the western edge of British settlement in the new world, where *Wacousta* is set, the view is similarly limited: "Even at the present day, along that line of remote country we have selected for the theatre of our labours, the garrisons are both few in number and weak in strength, and evidence of culti-vation is seldom to be found in any distance in the interior; so that all beyond a certain extent of clearing, continued along the banks of the lakes and rivers, is thick, impervious, rayless forest, the limits of which have never yet been explored, perhaps, by the natives themselves" (6). Despite Richardson's efforts, very little of this new world can be seen – very little of it is intelligible to either the people who are in it or those who are looking at it from a distance. The limited area from which the fog and the forest have been pushed back by the force of Richardson's vision and will is merely a narrow strip along the waterways: either could easily roll over it again.

At this point Richardson, having visually set the scene, moves to the political and cultural context of British, French, American, and native conflict in the new world, which causes him to repeat his earlier image of imperviousness, but with a particular emphasis: "Proceeding westward from [Detroit], and along the tract of country that diverged from the banks of the Lakes Huron, Sinclair, and Michigan, all traces of that partial civilization were again lost in impervious wilds, tenanted only by the fiercest of the Indian tribes, whose homes were principally along the banks of that greatest of American waters, the Lake Superior, and in the country surrounding the isolated fort of Michillimackinac, the last and most remote of the European fortresses in Canada" (9). The emptiness of that surrounding imperviousness is changed now: it is not simply the forest that threatens to engulf settlement and civilization but the Indians, immediately characterized by Richardson as hostile, treacherous, crafty, and politic (10), whom the forest hides. Richardson continues with a short analysis of French Canadian and English relations after the conquest and a sketch of "a few of the most prominent scenes more immediately before us" (12), the fort and town of Detroit as they appear in 1763, when the novel's action takes place. Even that description is qualified by historical conditions: he concludes the chapter by explaining how Detroit looks now at the time of writing and how both it and Michillimackinac were involved in the War of 1812, the fort at Detroit being destroyed by the British to prevent its use by the Americans. Again, Richardson has to place the new world not only geographically and visually but historically and personally as well. The pressure to do that is indicative of the instability of the new world; the world of his own creation threatens to disappear without the repeated reinforcement of historical record and personal authority.

The sense of threat that defines Richardson's imagination and his sense of the new world defines his text.[2] In this text, and in his other new world novels, it is apparent how close Richardson is to losing control. As the savages drop shrieking from the trees and the military formation moves backwards into the fort, it is clear that something has gone wrong in Richardson's imaginative transition to the new world. Richardson's problem is of language and structure, of content and context. His experience does not fit with the literary conventions he tries to use. His earlier European novels, *Ecarté* and *Frascati's*,[3] succeed to some extent at least because he knows both his setting and his material, and neither poses intellectual, personal, or formal problems for him. Not so in North America. The experience of the War of 1812 is Richardson's own, and he is able to transpose that to the Ponteac rebellions rather neatly. What is not so neat is the accommodation he attempts between that material and the new world Gothic romance and Indian/adventure novel, with the familiar themes of love gone wrong and honour betrayed diverging strenuously from those of new world savagery and violent cultural confrontation. In *Wacousta* Richardson's preoccupations centre on disorder, upheaval, trauma, and violence. He attempts to control that disorder by imposing upon it the formations of kinship and the military, but those structures disintegrate before the threats of the competing orders of the Indian tribes and the forests surrounding the Great Lakes. The genealogical metaphor breaks down quickly as family members are separated by death and distance or by military decorum, and romantic relationships are shaded by homosexuality, voyeurism, miscegenation, violence, and rape. The plots, characters, and ideas Richardson brings from the Gothic novel and from Scott's historical romances simply do not function when they are displaced.[4] Similarly, his ideals of military men and behaviour and of civilized human nature go awry in the North American context and are likewise sensationalized: the fort commander is a tyrant; a military court martial is a murder; and the savagery of a former British officer surpasses that of the natives of North America. The failure of the discursive construction of place and culture is echoed in the textual construction, and speaks of the gap between the experience of the place and the language available to describe it.

Kinship relations are integrally involved in *Wacousta*'s plot: all the principal European characters, who belong in some sense to the British military, have close familial ties. The originating event that motivates the plot is Reginald Morton's betrayal by his fellow officer, who marries the woman Morton loves. When the conflict is transferred to the new world, Morton's – now Wacousta's – planned revenge has grown to include Colonel de Haldimar's entire family in North America as well as the British garrisons at Detroit and Michillimackinac, which the colonel and his brother command: the conflict between individuals has changed registers and become a war between races and cultures. Kinship relations thus overlap with the public sphere. As well, the roles within the De Haldimar family reflect their public roles: the two sons are their father's military subordinates, while the daughter is the focus of the struggle between De Haldimar and Wacousta, as her mother was. If kinship defines the action by providing the parameters of the revenge plot, it might be expected to function positively; in this context, however, it seems simply to cause De Haldimar to demand an even more rigid observance of military procedure and protocol since, if the fort is overwhelmed, he has a great deal to lose. His overreaction to the Frank Halloway incident, eliciting Halloway's confession with a promise of amnesty and then executing him almost immediately, appears to demonstrate a lack of judgment and justice rather than the objective behaviour required in an incident in which his own son is involved.

In any interpretation the genealogical imperative is disturbed and refused: in *Wacousta* only Frederick and Madeline survive from the two De Haldimar families, and in the novel's sequel, *The Canadian Brothers*, the family is wiped out completely during the 1812 war in fulfilment of Ellen Halloway's curse. In that novel the war between the fragments of the two European societies transplanted to North America is figured in the relationships between the Grantham brothers, descendants of the De Haldimars, and Jeremiah Desborough, a descendant of Wacousta and Ellen: one Grantham kills the other, and Desborough kills the survivor. The Indians are loyal supporters of the British military, while the savage element is provided by another white man gone Indian, the offspring of Wacousta and Ellen. The genealogical metaphor is dysfunctional in both texts: the representatives of the British Empire, the two De Haldimar brothers, can neither secure this new world territory militarily nor establish a social, civil order through their offspring.

If the De Haldimar family relationships are complicated by their public function, the children's romantic alliances are correspondingly mixed. The model of European culture is the collection of relationships within the De Haldimar family. The triangular relationships and suggestions of incest and homosexuality in the text have been noticed by other critics[5] and point up Richardson's fascination with ordering structures, particularly as they are altered in the new world. Charles and Sir Valletort are extremely close, and grow closer when they can share Clara as sister and wife: Charles courts and wins Valletort for his sister, and Valletort loves both Clara and Charles for their similarities in body and character.[6] The men's relationship is parallelled by that between Clara and her cousin Madeline, who later marries Clara's brother Frederick. That relationship is triangular also, as Madeline is rescued from the Indian camp by Frederick's native lover Oucanasta, who betrays her own people to save Frederick and the garrison at Detroit. Oucanasta apparently recognizes the impossibility of an interracial marriage and sacrifices her own happiness for Frederick's, while Frederick's and Madeline's marriage, the one union that at least appears to have a future within the novel, remains strictly within the limits of the family and the British military system. The mixing of public and private orders is an indication not only of Richardson's attraction to seemingly reliable ordering structures but his recognition of their inability to contain the change that occurs in human beings and their relationships in the new world.

As the romantic relationships in the novel overlap with family bonds, so too are they mixed with intercultural considerations: the relationship between Oucanasta and Frederick is the major case in point. A gulf of silence extends across the cultures in that relationship, and in the larger intercultural dynamic in the novel. While titillating the reader with the suggestion of a sexual relationship between Frederick and Oucanasta, Richardson shows it to be impossible. Unlike many of his historical counterparts, Frederick does not seriously attempt a private sexual relationship with Oucanasta, and a public, permanent one is forbidden by their respective cultures. Oucanasta guides Frederick to safe locations in the forest for their meetings, but Frederick's presence there appropriates her place. In attempting to convince her that he values her devotion, he asks her to save the woman of his own culture who will take the place with him that she herself wants. Oucanasta literally loses her balance as she enters Frederick's frame of discourse to respond:

"Oucanasta is but a weak woman, and her feet are not swift like those of a runner among the red skins; but what the Saganaw asks, for his sake she will try ... The pale girl shall lay her head on the bosom of the Saganaw, and Oucanasta will try to rejoice in her happiness."

In the fervour of his gratitude, the young officer caught the drooping form of the generous Indian wildly to his heart; his lips pressed hers, and during the kiss that followed, the heart of the latter bounded and throbbed, as if it would have passed from her own into the bosom of her companion.

Never was a kiss less premeditated, less unchaste ... On the whole, however, it was a most unfortunate and ill-timed kiss, and, as is often the case under such circumstances, led to the downfall of the woman. In the vivacity of his embrace, Captain de Haldimar had drawn his guide so far forward upon the log, that she lost her balance, and fell with a heavy and reverberating crash among the leaves and dried sticks that were strewed thickly around.   (260)

Aside from bringing the Indians down around them, which results in Frederick's capture, this incident says much about the relationship possible between the two cultures and the inevitably ambivalent space this second world society will ultimately occupy.[7] Oucanasta agrees to save the fort and Frederick's lover, whom she recognizes as his rightful mate, despite her own feelings for him. The white man does not enter native society, although it is clear that Oucanasta would welcome him on a personal basis; Frederick takes it over for his own purposes and treats Oucanasta as a romantic European hero would his heroine. As a result the native is forced into the European discourse, or effaced.

Ponteac is the only Indian character in the novel to articulate a native point of view and act upon it. In the deliberately inconclusive meeting in the council chamber, which will require the second meeting and opportunity to invade the fort, Ponteac asks questions to which there is no good answer: "Why did the Saganaw come into the country of the red skins? ... Why did they take our hunting grounds from us? Why have they strong places encircling the country of the Indians, like a belt of wampum round the waist of a warrior?" (196). He also explains how the Europeans have caused the native aggression: "If the settlers of the Saganaw have fallen ... it is because they did not keep their faith with the red skins. When they came weak, and were not yet secure in their strong holds, their tongues were smooth and full of soft words; but when they became strong under the protection of their thunder, they no longer treated the red skins as their friends, and they laughed at them for letting them come into their country" (198). Richardson's early description of the natives as hostile, treacherous, crafty, and politic could well apply to the Europeans in the new world. His neither/nor positioning is obvious: he allows Ponteac to indict European imperialism and justify the native response, but he also allows Oucanasta and her brother to betray their own people, thereby gaining the approval of the European power structure within the novel. Richardson's ambivalence regarding the two cultures is expressed in Wacousta, who, in going Indian and living out his old world revenge in the guise of a new world savage, enacts more brutality and provokes more terror than any "real" Indian could.

Richardson attempts to use the military as another structural model for the developing European society in North America, but that model too is dysfunctional. The fort at Detroit under De Haldimar's command is vulnerable and insecure: the colonel is morally corrupt in his betrayals of Reginald Morton in Scotland and Frank Halloway in British North America, while his authoritarian and inflexible attitude towards both his children and his men threatens the fort's security. The men resent his rebuke of Valletort for firing at Wacousta and indict his treatment of Halloway. Those who have sufficient rank to express their judgment do so: Valletort is ready to "resign or exchange" (45) his posting, and Frederick must leave the fort against his father's orders to gain the information that will save it. The corruption filters down from the commanding officer to cause dissatisfaction and disobedience among the men and to shake their confidence in themselves and the British military system they represent. In the opening chapter the shouts in the dark, the intruder within the fort, and the shots fired at shadows underline the fact that the British garrison's attempt to control the new world setting with military order is a failure. Outside the fort the troops are commanded into the hollow square formation, an unwitting symbol of the garrison's lack of substance; when they are not in the square, they are ordered to march backwards. Richardson makes the most of one such scene in which the troops attempt to regain the fort:

Taking advantage of the terror produced, by this catastrophe, in the savages, Captain Erskine caused the men bearing the corpse to retreat, with all possible expedition, under the ramparts of the fort. He waited until they got nearly half way, and then threw forward the wheeling sections, that had covered this movement, once more into single file, in which order he commenced his retreat. Step by step, and almost imperceptibly, the men paced backwards, ready, at a moment's notice, to reform the square ... From [the bomb-proof] a galling fire, mingled with the most hideous yells, was now kept up; and the detachment, in their slow retreat, suffered considerably.   (63–4)

He adds the element of the grotesque as Donellan's scalped body rolls off the stretcher in this nerve-wrackingly slow retreat, and the men struggle to save it and themselves. The hollow square is used again for Frank Halloway's trial and sentencing and exemplifies the falseness and worthlessness of the military institution, as well as the illusory and unsustaining nature of the cultural construction that the British are trying to impose on the new world.

As a construct to impose and preserve meaning De Haldimar's military strategy is inappropriate and inadequate to its task: he can defend neither the fort nor the men, and punishes the act that saves them. That system should make the North American experience of a British soldier – Richardson's own experience – intelligible, but it does not. Halloway's end prefigures Richardson's personal discovery of the military's inadequacies. The breakdown of the military model he records corresponds to the breakdown of discourse that he encounters when he tries to write about the new world. The gap between the old and new world discourses locates Richardson in the transitional moment in which a full and complete possession of either is impossible. If language is a tool with which a world can be textually constructed, it also constructs and exposes difference, separation, and absence (Ashcroft, Griffiths, Tiffin 44). Richardson can provide the literal details of the setting and landscape, but he has difficulty understanding and communicating just what those details mean. Figuratively, the bridge where Halloway is executed, Clara murdered, and Charles and Wacousta die represents the impossibility of bridging the gap between the North American indigenous culture and the European culture without horrific amounts of conflict and bloodshed, if at all. The characters in the work who die there do indeed fall into the chasm, but Richardson is teetering on its edge as well. He is determined to shape his Canadian material into a form given him by a revenge plot and type characters, but his literary conventions are inadequate to deal with content so far beyond the bounds of the familiar and the understandable. This formal dilemma causes his fiction to grow increasingly out of control. His discursive system cannot support the absolute horror he feels as he realizes the void and silence that he, and British North America, are facing. The imminent annihilation of the two British forts in *Wacousta* has far greater consequences than the loss of military advantage and a number of British lives. The presence of the British is less secure than the possibility of their absence, and of the non-being to which British North America and Richardson himself will be subject if the European presence that lends it intelligibility disappears.

The Europeans may well be swallowed up by the new world. The fear and confusion inside the fort is palpable and, in a striking echo of Diaz's reaction noted earlier, reality is indistinguishable from imagination: "De Haldimar looked again. – 'I do begin to fancy I see something,' he replied; 'but so confusedly and indistinctly, that I know not whether it be not merely an illusion of my imagination'" (29). The "illusion of the imagination" in Diaz's experience is translated into a textual convention. In Richardson's it becomes paralysing fear and potential madness. When the troops leave the fort to recover the body at the dugout and to execute Frank Halloway at the bridge, the men are exposed and in terrible danger, not so much from a recognized enemy but from the real or *imagined* threat that might be lurking beyond the edges of the forest surrounding the fort and its island of cleared space. Their imagination makes that threat worse and allows the Indian enemy to assume Wacousta's "powerful proportions and gigantic stature" (80) and become a "legion of devils" (49). In this nightmare all circumstances are equally unreal and illusory: madness is an all too likely response to the European inability to discern an intelligible (and familiar) reality.

Richardson and his British characters are threatened by liminality. They disappear from the view of the old world into the impenetrable forest, connected to their former place and state of being by the water route through the Great Lakes, which is periodically blocked by the Indians. That connection is tenuous and fragile; they are not restored to their former lives and must struggle so as not to disappear from the new world setting as well. The threat of liminality registers as absence in the text. The colonel is essentially absent from family relationships and as a figure to inspire trust and respect in his men. Frederick disappears into absence and invisibility when he leaves the fort and is beyond the limits of military behaviour for disobeying orders, feared dead, assumed killed – completely absent from human intercourse when outside the ramparts. He spends that time surrounded by forest, wrapped in an Indian blanket, and hidden in a hollow tree – further layers of invisibility and absence that he must impose on himself to gain access to the Indian camp and some knowledge of the other culture. Wacousta, too, is periodically and strikingly absent: as he changes races and continents, he is lost to the culture he leaves behind. The humiliated and court-martialled Reginald Morton disappears from the British military and social realms to become a Scottish renegade. When he reappears in North America to fight for the French and try to kill Frederick on the Plains of Abraham, he has been lost to his former life without yet possessing the possibility of moving on to another; at his transformation into the Indian warrior his stature has increased and his skin darkened, physical changes that are registered in his change of name.

The most prominent absences in *Wacousta*, however, are suffered by Frank Halloway and his wife Ellen. While Frederick is wrapped in the hollow tree, Frank Halloway stands in the centre of the hollow square and defends himself against the charge of treason not simply by explaining his part in Frederick's disappearance but by revealing his previous name and recounting the history of his previous life. He tells the story of his honourable birth as Reginald Morton, his family's respectable position, and their opposition to his relationship with Ellen; stripped of income and home, and known as Frank Halloway, he joins the military and performs exemplarily as a means of earning a living and preserving some decency and honour in a suddenly disorderly life. Halloway's defence is intended to give him visibility and intelligibility, but it does not because the prevailing power structure will not recognize it. The centre of power in the novel insists on its own discursive construction: the transition to the new world so threatens the military construct that Halloway's history and military record cannot be allowed to answer the charge of treason. Halloway speaks into a void where his words do not mean because the frame of discourse he uses for his defence is not recognized by the power that could grant it meaning. His words fall silent at his feet, and he follows them into the void. His execution takes place outside the fort – his uniform seized, his wife ordered to remain inside the fort, his not unreasonable request for delay until Frederick's imminent arrival ignored. The things that gave an intelligible meaning to Frank Halloway are taken from him, just as those that had functioned similarly for him as Reginald Morton had been earlier removed. His physical death is anti-climactic, although Richardson plays it out in a dramatic scene with Frederick, whose words could save Halloway's life, approaching in the distance (150). Halloway disappears from North America, just as Reginald Morton had from England, but this time with no possibility of a reappearance: the ordering structure that should save him cannot. Old world discourse does not contain meaning or guarantee survival in this setting.

Ellen Halloway too is a liminal figure throughout the text, and in a more significant way than her husband. She suffers the loss of family connection and name with him, but her situation in North America is much more extreme: his unjust trial and execution take place in some relation to a structure of meaning, inadequate as it is in North America, a relation that never exists for Ellen in the new world. The original dislocation from her place and her identity becomes permanent as she fails to reconnect to any other context: "I am not Ellen Halloway: they said so; but it is not true. My husband was Reginald Morton: but he went for a soldier, and was killed; and I never saw him more" (437). She enters the liminal phase in what should be a temporary stage but does not re-emerge: there is nowhere for her to go. The resulting psychic damage is permanent and irreversible. Ellen is truly between worlds as one of a number of anonymous and invisible military wives inside the fort, the disguised drummer-boy accompanying the procession to the bridge for her husband's execution, and the madwoman who curses De Haldimar and his descendants over her husband's corpse. In a very real sense Ellen Halloway does not survive her husband.

Richardson depicts Ellen as a hysteric in her distress – her shrieks startle, her hair streams – which may be more or less conventional treatment of a woman of sensibility in distress. What is not conventional, however, is that a woman of sensibility would be in this distress, in this place. Richardson detaches Ellen from the fringes of British North American society when he has her leap on top of Halloway's coffin and declare the curse upon De Haldimar and his descendants: "if there be spared one branch of thy detested family, may it only be that they may be reserved for some death too horrible to be conceived!" (154). With this act she steps metaphorically into Wacousta's camp, withdrawing herself from the garrison and its representatives, whom she condemns, and pledging herself to revenge. Like Wacousta, Ellen has gone Indian, moving distinctly out of the European context and the limits it understands and imposes on behaviour into something unknown and, to British North Americans, empty – of reason, intelligence, rules, morality. She has moved out of the discursive system in which Richardson and his readers could understand her. The only development Richardson can provide for her after she has fallen backwards into Wacousta's arms and been carried off is the madness the text has threatened. In Wacousta's tent in the forest she is withdrawn and incoherent, her eyes wild, her face blank, and her movements mechanical (433). Her reaction is clearly not the result of white womanhood's violation by a savage but of the accumulation of violent displacements she has experienced. Her absence, first from her old world home and then from European society in the new world, is both literal and figurative. She disappears into the forest with the epitome of the "savage" just as she disappeared from her personal and social position in Britain when she married and her name was changed. In fact she is literally absent from the text the moment Wacousta carries her away, and only reappears momentarily, as a figure of secondary interest, when Richardson shows Clara about to be raped by Wacousta.

In what we do see of Ellen in the forest she has clearly rejected her identity as a European woman acting within the structures of her culture: when Clara tries to steal her knife to free Valletort and enable their escape, Ellen prevents her, apparently unaware that she has grasped the blade of the knife to do so (500). By that act she declares herself an enemy of the Europeans and a savage in their eyes, as Wacousta has become. Her intense loyalty to each husband named Reginald Morton is consistent with Richardson's ideas of female character, but the situation goes awry when those Mortons change continents, identities, and loyalties: Ellen must change also. This introduces new ambiguities, a difficulty Richardson avoids by avoiding the character. After this scene Ellen is absent and unmentioned until the last line of the novel, which prepares for its sequel: "As for poor Ellen Halloway, search had been made for her, but she never was heard of afterwards" (543). Richardson is obviously fascinated by the cluster of issues this strange creature he has created represents, but she is not easy for him to categorize and he leaves her position unexamined. The madness he projects on to her is his way of expressing the fact that she is no longer of this world and of encoding a position he cannot develop or understand. Ellen enacts the results of displacement, loss, and terror that threaten everyone in the novel. She is the ghost in *Wacousta* and figures much more largely in her absence than Richardson may have realized or intended.

Richardson's vision of the accommodation of the European to the new world culture is blocked by his preconceptions of the people and the place. The warrior Wacousta is a stock character, and terribly European despite his disguise. In the scene in the tent with Clara, Wacousta's alternation between the new world savage and the old world Reginald Morton shows that his identity is not firmly in place: the effective identifying relationship between self and place (Ashcroft, Griffiths, Tiffin 9) has been destroyed by the move to the new world. In response to Clara's tears and entreaties Wacousta obeys "one of these rapid transitions of feeling, for which he was remarkable" (460) and becomes again the old world gentleman relating the narrative of his betrayal, which he must do to justify his new world savagery: personal history again attempts explanation and defence. Wacousta's silences between the narrativizing of his past and the violence of his intentions towards Clara point up the gaps Richardson encounters when he attempts to write of the British North American wilderness. Between Wacousta's conflicting identities as the wronged man of honour and the ignoble savage, between his discursive systems, is the silence Richardson falls into when he has no fitting form for experience. Richardson does not know if one can leave the old world behind or if one can become a part of the new world. What is most revealing is that Wacousta does not enact his savagery by raping Clara:[8] the threat is what is necessary for the suspense in the text. He remains bound by the conventions of honour that have informed his revenge against De Haldimar from the beginning.

The sexual aggression of the pseudo-savage figures Wacousta's and Richardson's attempts to demonstrate power and reassert control not simply in the male/female context but in the imperial context as well: both Wacousta and Richardson have lost their control by leaving the imperial centre. In this scene Wacousta is in the position of power because the representatives of the imperial centre, the garrison and the De Haldimars, are similarly displaced and even more maladapted to the margin than he is. As well, the

sexual element, with its attendant discourse of power, is a continuing preoccupation for Richardson. The "savage" male enacting
vengeance and violence on the female representative of the coloniz-
ing culture is a fitting metaphor of the confusion and disorder
Richardson faced when trying to fit himself into the colonial context as a member of neither the imperial culture nor the settler
society, and is symptomatic of his displacement and marginalization
as well as of the chaos and unintelligibility that attend his presence
in the new world.

The silences in Richardson's text occur in the gaps between the
forms he wants to use and the experience he wants to express, and
are pointed up, paradoxically, by noise: the rattle of guns, shrieks
of Ellen, and whoops of savages mark the absence of meaning that
attends dishonourable acts and the fall into disorder. Absence and
silence frequently figure as disguise in the novel: Richardson's
characters sometimes cannot speak because they do not know who
they are. As Ellen moves from daughter to wife to drummer-boy
to widow to concubine, her social and sexual identity crumbles and
she falls into silence. Wacousta's silences fall between the conflicting
systems of discourse he tries to use in his simultaneous presentation
of himself as the wronged Reginald Morton and the Indian renegade. Frederick wears his subordinate Donellan's clothing when he
leaves the fort at night, which leads to a further confusion of
identities when Donellan is discovered dead in Frederick's uniform.
Frederick's retreats into the dark, beneath a blanket, and within a
tree all hide his presence and reinforce his silence, a silence that
saves his life and causes Donellan's and Halloway's deaths. Two
Claras are confronted by Wacousta in two oases; there are two
forts, two miniature portraits, two Reginald Mortons, two perilous
quests out of the ordinary civilized realm of order and common
sense across a border abyss, two worlds reflecting each other and
exposing disorder and chaos.[9] The proliferation of disguises and
double identities is Richardson's means of expressing his awareness
of the possibility of personal and social disintegration in the new
world and the insecure presence of both discursive constructions –
an extreme version of Tiffin's double vision. As identity and reality
become ever more difficult to discern, the moral ambiguities of the
new world experience are pointed up. The lines between the two
worlds of good and evil waver and fade as characters blur into one
another and each culture is seen to have its own strengths and

weaknesses. It becomes increasingly difficult to tell which is the realm of order and which chaos, while good and evil are problematic and highlight the contradictory tensions inherent in the new world (Hurley 67).

The absence of structure apparent in *Wacousta* is no less critical in the new world itself at the time Richardson sets his works there. Much of Richardson's difficulty in controlling *Wacousta* is caused by the setting. The problem of transferring European characters to a new world landscape is real when one's language, historical context, and literary tradition do not fit the experience that is to be shaped into literature. Richardson has difficulty placing his characters of sensibility into a framework of social and personal relationships. He also has trouble conceptualizing the landscape, and attempts to transfer characteristics of the old world landscape to the new, most strikingly in the parallel between the Scottish Highland oasis and the Indian camp. Clara Beverly is secreted in the idyllic oasis by her father to protect her from the outside world and preserve her innocence; this intention is violated as Reginald Morton carries her away through the chasms and crags that separate it from the known world. Clara's innocence is fragile and may be largely inexperience; succumbing quickly to De Haldimar's seduction, she betrays Morton's love and helps to destroy his career and reputation without visible guilt or remorse.

The oasis, then, is not sufficiently distanced from ordinary society in kind or in space: Morton discovers it during an afternoon of hunting and often visits after his daily military duty, while the elderly woman servant regularly negotiates the passage through the rocks to the town below. Richardson does not allow a permanent withdrawal: the Highlands are not secure from the imperial forces of "civilization." Similarly, the British do not see the order, shape, and definition of the Indian camp in the forest, another oasis and defensive structure as well planned and better protected than their own:

the encampment of the investing Indians ... was, as has been shown, situate in a sort of oasis close within the verge of the forest, and (girt by an intervening underwood which Nature, in her caprice, had fashioned after the manner of a defensive barrier) embraced a space sufficient to contain the tents of the fighting men, together with their women and children. This, however, included only the warriors and inferior chiefs. The

tents of the leaders were without the belt of underwood, and principally
distributed at long intervals on that side of the forest which skirted the
open country towards the river; forming, as it were, a chain of external
defences, and sweeping in a semi-circular direction round the more dense
encampment of their followers.   (431)

Instead they see it as the source of savagery, chaos, and their own
annihilation. The camp is not in the human sphere but in the
enigmatic territory of monsters: when Wacousta, Frederick, Ellen,
Clara, and Valletort disappear into the forest, they are lost to the
view of the fort and enveloped in a chaos in which only the worst
and most unimaginable things can happen. The natives are clichéed
savages – leaping out of the bomb shelter, shrieking across the plain,
dropping from the trees on to the deck of the schooner – rather
than members of a planned and coherent community. Although
Richardson does not make the point explicitly, it is obvious that
the native oasis too has ideals worth protecting from the corrupting
influence of the outside world, which in this case is the European
colonial power with its appetite for territory and influence. In both
cases the isolation of the oasis must eventually give way to the
pressures of so-called civilization and military strength.

The parallel between settings becomes more complex when the
British fort, surrounded by its interval of cleared space, is consid-
ered as another oasis. It is neither safe nor secure, however – the
competing oasis of the Indians threatens to overwhelm it, although
it will eventually be beaten back and itself destroyed. In the mean-
time, though, the forest setting of *Wacousta* is not the site of
sojourn that the Highland oasis seemed to be: this is not a place
these British gentlepeople are simply visiting with the return to their
homes both promised and possible. The Sinclair River and the lake
that lies before the fort at Michillimackinac are not a shining portal
through which the Europeans trapped there can return to their own
world (286–7), although they (and Richardson) may hope so. They
are *here*, although they may not know where here is, and if they
are to survive they must impose their own structures and values on
the setting, which requires the destruction of the native order and
the construction of their own in its place.

The European concept of human nature is another problem of
definition and potential disintegration in Richardson's new world,

and linked to the question of place. Richardson blurs the boundaries between civilization and nature, noble and savage, primarily
in the figure of Wacousta. The metaphors of the wild man and
noble savage were commonly used to identify what resisted conventional systems of classification, a crucially necessary function
when a culture encounters something that eludes normal expectations and experience (White "Fetish" 122). North American natives
had to be translated into a European system of values and norms
and, in their perceived absence of speech discussed earlier, fulfilled
one aspect of the definition of the wild man. The myth of the noble
savage, embodying the tension between the noblest qualities of the
Christian and the non-Christian, primitivism and archaism, nature
and convention, was applied to the natives of North America as it
had been earlier to other races, and did not encourage an understanding of the indigenous population of North America; European
acts of brutality and ignorance could be sanctioned when directed
against wild men and savages rather than human beings.[10] As the
image of wildness is fictionalized and becomes an instrument of
intracultural criticism, Richardson's *Wacousta* comes into focus;
deliberately or not, Richardson's example of a civilized culture –
the British in North America – undercuts that culture's assessment
of its own virtues. One of its members is simply using the new
world as an arena for his own ends. Although Wacousta is obsessed
with revenge, it is revenge within the structure of European culture:
he is not a savage, noble or otherwise, at all. De Haldimar's betrayal
of Morton, which provides the plot of the novel and causes
Morton's transformation, occurs when the British Army is attempting to control Highlanders in Scotland. Richardson does not refer
directly to the military or political objectives of the British campaigns but makes several references to "the disturbed nature of the
times": the eighteenth- and nineteenth-century conceptions of the
savage and the civilized, in both old and new worlds, are implicit.

The debate over human nature shades in *Wacousta* into the
question of the kind of intercultural relations possible in the new
world. Part of Richardson's ambiguity on this point is the historical
and cultural ambiguity of white settler societies, which we now
recognize: the culture is defined not only by the relationship
between European cognitive codes and the impulse to create an
independent local identity, but as well by its role as the colonizer

of the indigenous population while still colonized itself by Europe. Eventually all the principal "civilized" European characters, with the exception of Frederick and Madeline, disappear into either the gorge or a grave. Richardson leaves the problem of race relations in Frederick's and Madeline's hands and apparently wants to feel some confidence in their ability to bridge the two cultures: Oucanasta and her brother remain valued friends of the family, while the rest of the Indians blend into an anonymous and affable mass. Ironically and significantly it is the European position that is extremely precarious in Richardson's view.[11] Throughout the novel Richardson has used the bridge joining the banks of the river and the Indian and British territories to show just how unlikely any cultural interaction except war will be. Attack, death, and murder all occur there, along with many of Richardson's heightened effects: shrieks, threats, and curses, the wolf-dog lapping up "the blood and brains" (179) of Frank Halloway. In the meetings that occur elsewhere intercultural communication is ineffective or destructive. Intercultural relations are figured in a conflict of discourses very like those discussed by Greenblatt and Todorov: during the meeting in the council chamber each group uses ritual to conceal strategy; on the lake at Michillimackinac a message is delivered but misread; when he infiltrates the Indian camp, all Frederick is prepared to hear is the Indians' plan to surprise the fort, which he calls treachery.

Native culture and language do not register in Europe's discursive universe: Wacousta must explain to the colonel that "there are certain figures, as you are aware, that, traced on bark, answer the same purpose among the Indians with the European language of letters" (523). The British recognize only their own forms and their own right and power of cultural domination; the natives' grunts and war whoops and the (French) Canadians' dialect are neither understood nor admitted into the discursive construction of power. The natives and previously conquered European settlers are colonized and excluded by language; as the British determine what can be communicated and by what means, the power of the pen becomes cultural and imperial domination. That discursive control is both tenuous and essential for European survival in the new world: the existence of the fort at Michillimackinac depends on the message carried to it by two white men through a wilderness of forest and warring Indians.

Frederick and Madeline are left presiding over a very precarious peace: Richardson does not follow up the cultural conflict, but not because it has been resolved. The revenge plot takes over from what could have been an examination of the attempts at cultural integration in the new world. In choosing that focus Richardson acts within predictable limits. If the native culture were to be taken seriously, it would have to be seen and presented as an alternative to the white. However flawed the white culture, the native culture was not, in nineteenth-century North America, a possible alternative: making the Indian backdrop anything more would have been not only complex but a violation of the premises of popular culture (Berkhofer 98). Richardson is not willing to introduce that kind of ambiguity into his text. Although he criticizes white values and actions, his comments are personal rather than historical: historical judgments would have been against his own experience and would have risked alienating his audience. He fears the breakdown of the European construction while recognizing it is not ideal, but sees no way to ensure European survival in the new world other than by insisting on its reinforcement.

Oucanasta and her brother are neither credible representatives of the native structure nor effective intercultural intermediaries because they act for the Europeans against their own people: the possibility of reconciliation between the opposites of wilderness and civilization requires betrayal. As representatives of the other culture, Frederick is limited by the military structure that informs his thinking and behaviour, and Madeline, one assumes, will go little beyond her curatorial interest in Indian artifacts. Richardson provides his novel with a happy and optimistic ending regarding the future of the European settlement at Detroit. That ending, however, is not entirely consistent with the situation he has presented – Fort Michillimackinac has been burned to the ground and the British presence on the upper lakes removed – and leaves his Europeans at significant risk. In *The Canadian Brothers*, set some fifty years later, the lives of his principal characters are no more secure, but this time the threat comes from other Europeans, while the natives have been diminished to physical and cultural curiosities. European life in the new world is no more secure in 1812 than in 1763; the violence that the new world seems to allow, if not provoke, destroys even the generation born there, as Richardson himself was.

Wacousta shows that Richardson has great difficulty assimilating the difference between the settled European place he experienced in his early adulthood and North America – unsettled, unspoken, un-understood. His problem is particularly acute because he is born in a new world where social and other values are determined by old world structures; he is at a double disadvantage because, although he is not firmly attached to the new culture in the new place, neither does he have memories of a former place. He is born too soon, before his culture has made itself at home in the new world; in Partridge's terms, there are as yet no home-made legends for the European population. Richardson is both exile and alien[12] and, as such, participates in the cultural and discursive invention of Canada. Richardson, writing on his western frontier, and nineteenth-century British North America itself are caught in the historical process that prevents a full accommodation to the place or the time: neither the author nor the developing nation can successfully create what Harrison calls "an imaginative framework to point the order and keep out the chaos."[13]

Given that reality is socially constructed by the human consciousness in language, Richardson's problem in articulating his experience is not so surprising. What is perhaps more surprising is his qualified success. Within this context it is clear that Richardson reacted in a comprehensible and predictable manner upon finding himself within a fragment of European culture transplanted to the new world. He was unable to see his situation within the framework of the historical process, nor could he realize that art does not reflect nature but contemporary thought structures. Richardson's rigidity about what he allows into and what he keeps out of his work is typical of the cultural dogmatism of fragment cultures.[14] He tries to work almost completely within the modes of order of his culture, which he hopes will keep out the chaos and give intelligibility, coherence, and meaning to his work for himself and his contemporaries. The problematic incidents in the text occur where those modes of order are not yet in place. In Dennis Lee's terms, for Richardson "home" is ambiguous: "the colonial writer does not have words of his own" (162). The undermining silence beneath the words the colonial powers have provided is present, from Richardson's time to our own: we understand the temptation to terror in Richardson's text, as well as the impetus for Watson's and Kroetsch's investigations of language and Urquhart's interrogations of historical and fictional discourses.

John Richardson and *Wacousta* are dramatic examples of the impossibility of a culture's attempt to articulate itself in literature when its discursive structure is not yet in place. *Wacousta* threatens to unravel before his and our eyes because of the matrix of circumstances under which it is written. Richardson's personal and social world is radically in question, as was British North America at this time in history. He falls silent or deflects the reader's attention from problematic subjects not because he does not want to deal with them, but because he cannot. Possessing neither the structural nor the historical framework to accommodate the fundamental questions of the new society, he lacks more profoundly the language in which those questions could be posed. He is very much under the pressure of history and tradition, which determine the discourses that are available to him.

Richardson takes his position on the bridge – between cultures, identities, realities. In his world, horror has to be viewed with detachment to save sanity (Duffy "Loyalist" 46), so much detachment that he can actually describe his novel in these terms: "Neither the lover of amorous adventure, nor the admirer of witty dialogue, should dive into these pages. Room for the exercise of the invention might, it is true, be found; but ours is a tale of sad reality, and our heroes and heroines figure under circumstances that would render wit a satire upon the understanding, and love a reflection upon the heart. Within the bounds of probability have we, therefore, confined ourselves" (440). He tries to adopt the stance of detached observer and narrator, not unlike Madeline, because he needs the distance. If forced into contact, by his definition beyond those bounds of probability, his shock would be as great as hers. North American experience remains discontinuous and inexplicable until Richardson can distance himself from what he has seen and fit it into some larger pattern of historic or symbolic meaning.[15] He remains fascinated by the line between honourable and dishonourable conduct, conventional and unconventional sexual relations, human and inhuman nature, civilization and wilderness. He constantly pushes against the limits of the way things are understood and written in his time, but when he goes beyond them he is apt to swerve into the excesses of his later novels.

Richardson is mired in the middle passage,[16] stranded between a familiar, comprehensible order and a new world whose horrors figure only vaguely in his imagination and are therefore all the more terrifying: "When the eye turned wood-ward, it fell heavily, and without interest, upon a dim and dusky point, *known* to enter upon savage scenes and unexplored countries" (286; emphasis added). Richardson does not really *know* what lies within the forest. Like the schooner on the Sinclair River, he must negotiate an extremely circumscribed passage: if he hesitates, or leans to either side, the surrounding unnamed and unknown terrors will overwhelm him. His characters remain in that middle passage with him, and his novel about the new world can show only the extremely precarious position of European culture as it attempts the transition from old to new world. In Europe the structures of meaning retain content and visibility: the only horrors in his European works are losses of honour and reputation caused by transgressions against a fixed social order. When those structures are transported and set down in the fragment culture in North America, they sustain nothing. They cannot be used as a basis on which to build a new society that would mirror the old because the new world demands their radical interrogation, which results in their collapse. Richardson's attempt to frame his North American experience in fiction is only partially successful, in either personal or literary terms; it is, however, tremendously revealing of the cultural and discursive invention of the new world.

CHAPTER THREE

Frederick Philip Grove: "No Language of My Own"

Frederick Philip Grove participates personally and intellectually in the new world's discursive construction. That activity is, for him, slightly out of focus, since he is primarily concerned with constructing his own person in that place; for his readers it is central and integral to his work. To use the metaphor of binocular vision, Grove has only one lens focused; the reader, using two, reads Grove's negotiation of two lives as both background and foreground to his negotiation of two worlds. While Richardson explores, with some foreboding, the limits beyond which new world discourse will fail, Grove cannot afford to do so: his existence is conditional upon the stability of the new world. Grove cannot wholly inhabit himself or his place because of the circumstances of his flight from Europe.[1] In many ways it would be convenient for him to be a new man in Canada, springing from nowhere on to the Canadian prairie, but the conditions caused by his abandonment of self and place require him to fill the gaps of his life and experience with fictions and disguises determined by his old world life.

Grove attempts to replace the cultural and discursive framework he has walked out of by creating a new one from the new world setting and from within himself, a difficult enough transaction without the complication of the doubled identity and denied past. His textual and cultural constructions are undermined by the threat of his personal absence, which he both asserts and denies every time he speaks and writes: his gulf of silence threatens personal annihilation. Precisely because of the particular conditions of his existence here, Grove and his work exhibit in startling clarity the predicament of the new world writer: he is suspended between the suddenly and decidedly unavailable discursive system of the old world and the equally inaccessible system of the new. He does not enjoy the objectivity or distance necessary to understand or articulate his position; in his own terms he is attempting to create a fiction of personal identity, but his attempt extends beyond his own person. Grove's transitional moment between discursive systems lasts his lifetime; Canada's transitional moment is displayed in the record of Grove's life and writing.

Like Richardson, Grove is faced with the imminent collapse of structures of meaning in the new world. His negotiation of the middle passage is extended, since the self he is trying to integrate into the new world society is not the self that existed in the old world: he is attempting a personal transformation in mid-passage. The negation of humanity experienced in the suspension between cultures threatens to become permanent for Grove: he has erased Felix Paul Greve, and the persona of Frederick Philip Grove that he has created in its place is in constant danger of disintegration. He determinedly and repeatedly writes himself and what he conceives to be his place into existence: the alternative is silence and absence. In one sense Grove's Canadian writing speaks more of him than of Canada, despite his reputation as Canada's prairie realist and the credit he received for giving voice to Canada, particularly to the Canadian west, and his own refusal of that function ("Apologia" 194). As Walter Pache has noted, there is a paradox in his canonization as a Canadian classic ("Perspectives" 18); in another and ironic sense, though, the conditions caused by his revision of his past make his speaking of Canada more significant than earlier critics have realized.

Grove's invention of his own new world is obsessively present in all his writing. The invention of the new world is complex for Grove; his peculiar position without a name or an identity save that of his own making require that invention to be personal and social, and the process to be conscious and foregrounded. His crisis of person and place is acutely apparent in his early letters, as J.J. Healy discusses in detail.[2] It is apparent as well in his autobiographical works, *A Search for America* and *In Search of Myself*, the account of his journeys in *Over Prairie Trails*, and the pioneer novels. His mixing of genres within the autobiographies and within his corpus is indicative of the discursive gap in which he was living and working. His life in the new world is a complex fiction in which a doubling of his two official identities, Greve and Grove, occurs repeatedly. Grove's necessity is to retain control over the Greve life: he denies that former existence but repeatedly draws on it for the history of the newer version of himself. And it is apparent from the knowledge of his life as Greve that even the so-called real past he draws upon in Europe is largely of his own creation;[3] his sense of himself as an established member of European social and literary circles is an ideal rather than a reality. The ironic results of this curiously doubled doubling are apparent throughout his Canadian writings.

We see in Grove's continuing study of self and of the external world – both landscape and social place – the processes by which he attempts to find the discourse that is authentic for both himself and the new world. Those processes are central to his writing and his life: he is involved in that examination on both public and private levels for as long as he is known to have been in Canada. His sense of personal identity is so fragile that it requires constant reinforcement, which takes much of his energy: it is logically the subject of his North American writing because it is in writing and in being a writer that his identity is consolidated. The acuity of his problem with individual identity, the shifting "I," shows in his work. North America, for Grove, is abstract: in some ways it has no reality for him (Healy 89). Individuality, too, has become an abstraction: that is one aspect of his loss. By defining the landscape in concrete terms Grove establishes the necessary distinction between the human being and the natural landscape, and constructs an identity he can place within the context of a shared humanity. In so doing he must define not only himself but the new cultural construction. That is a difficulty for him because it is a doubled necessity: to support and maintain the "I," he has to support and maintain the place in which the "I" now exists, precarious as that existence is.

Grove's determination to distinguish between himself and his place and to consolidate both causes his painstaking delineation of wind and waves, farms and roads, fog and snow in *Over Prairie Trails*. He works hard to maintain the division of "I" and "not-I" that he repeatedly asserts: the existence of a discrete personality can be proved only by contrast to the natural landscape and by both contrast and relatedness to other human beings. The western plain is strangely empty of individuals for Grove, inhabited only by larger-than-life figures – John Elliot, Abe Spalding, Niels Lindstedt – engaged in heroic tasks. History, too, is empty for him: he is deprived of his own European past, and Canada's does not register for him. Because of these conditions, certain characteristics overlap in his treatments of person and place. With the past rendered inaccessible, Grove, his pioneers, and Canada are oriented towards future possibility as land is cleared and farms and communities are established. Deprived of a particular social and historical order, Grove needs not to find a substitute but to participate in the construction of a new one, an act that conditions in western Canada in the early twentieth century allow.

Grove's fiction contains a remarkably accurate and detached analysis of his unique situation: "When I came from Europe, I came as an individual; when I settled down in America, at the end of my wanderings, I was a social man. My view of life, if now, at the end, I may use this word once more, had been, in Europe, historical, it had become, in America, ethical" (*America* 382). When Grove leaves his life in Europe he also leaves a highly specific individuality and past; what remains is a universalized human being in an abstract, ahistorical setting. As Healy puts it, he ceases to be an individual: the intact, coherent identity supported by past and place is replaced by a proposition (90). In the negotiation of the middle passage he leaves behind past, future, personal and social connectedness. In the new world he scrambles to reconstruct connections to people and place: he marries soon after his official arrival in Canada and assumes the respectable and visible community position of teacher and high-school principal. The social self is difficult for him to create and maintain, though, partly due to his feelings of isolation and failure as a writer; the connection to his imprecise and imperfect notions of the place in which he has landed is even more problematic.

The pressure of Grove's position is apparent in his battles with schoolteachers and trustees. When he writes to Isaak Warkentin in Germany, "*I have got* to win out" (Pacey, *Letters* 9), in a dispute over authority, he is literally speaking the truth. Grove no longer has distance, judgment, or proportion, and his behaviour is not unwarranted from a man who has lost so much: he has so little of Fred Grove in place that he can afford no flexibility (Healy 92). Not only must he define himself in opposition to the other, human or nature, but he must win: he stakes everything he is and has every time he asserts himself, his name, his position. Grove's self-generation is through self-control, as Spettigue points out ("Fanny Essler" 53); that self-control this early in his North American life is extremely fragile. Phil Branden's comment in *A Search for America*, that "nobody who is self-conscious can get away with the pretence that he is at ease" (21), expresses this tension and pressure. Because Grove's assertions are so fraught with risk, because his creation and placement of self are tentative, his writing can be only the dramatic presentation of generalized, social human beings working out ethical dilemmas (Healy 90). Sketching the outlines of individuals and society takes almost all his energy and effort. Struggling to maintain his existence beyond the liminality he enters when Felix Paul Greve "dies," Grove simply cannot negotiate the private, personal, historical realm. His repeated insistence that "I must be I" registers doubly and ironically when we realize that the construction and continual shoring up of that "I," which is literally not "I," is what he would recognize as his life's work. We recognize that his life's work extends beyond the "I." Peter Hulme's "alien and hostile world, where words, like actions, are improvised in a savage void, having no resonance beyond their immediate effect" (156), is Grove's. The lack of memory and narrative, which Hulme describes as a condition of colonialist discourse, is met by the identity Grove proposes and the setting in which he places it: in so far as Grove's constructions stand, Canada stands. What Healy calls his "rhetorical self-presentation" (101) is parallelled, allowed, and dependent on his rhetorical cultural presentation.

The nature of his break with the old world determines Grove's inability to perceive and conceive the new. He is, in fact, extremely old world oriented: he constantly compares, either explicitly or implicitly, the Canadian literary community to the circles in which he participated, or wanted to participate, in Europe. The new identity he creates for himself is an old world identity. This is partly, of course, for practical reasons: on the Canadian prairie in the 1910s he could not hide his Europeanness or a German accent, although he did deny his German nationality. He cannot deny the kind of past he has had or has wanted to have, however: his posited origins are aristocratic, cultured, and wealthy. Grove's audience is problematic for him precisely because he has no past: he has had two and lost them both by denying the Greve past that actually existed and substituting for it an imaginatively improved version. Grove is both aware of and controlled by the problem of his past as it complicates the construction of the new identity; the nature of the "I" is doubly uncertain as he eradicates the former past and uses parts of it to make a new one, thereby forcing himself into a historical and personal vacuum.

Grove's life is complicated by the fact that he has lost not only name and place but his first language as well: although he may have been reluctant to accept that inevitable loss, his North American writing is in English.[4] The disintegration of discourses is complete. In *In Search of Myself* he speaks of his social and linguistic isolation: "I felt an exile. I was an exile. I did not live among people of my own kind; among people who, metaphorically, spoke my language" (235). Of course, this is literally as well as metaphorically true for Grove, and for Phil in *A Search for America*. *A Search for America*, widely assumed in Grove's lifetime to be autobiographical, is so in a particular way: it is a textual construction of Grove's reconciliation to North America and a discursive construction of the place itself. In the novel Phil's language is not the English of North America nor the colloquial speech of the man from Simpson's. In a larger sense, though, the fact that both Phil and Grove have lost the ability to speak means that no discourse yet exists in the new world that could grant them meaning. Grove knows this: "I realized that I had at bottom no language which was peculiarly my own" (*Myself* 338). The raft-man Phil encounters is one of the silent and enigmatic old men recurring throughout Grove's work – John Elliot, Sam Clark, Sigurdsen, Mr Lund – who are deprived of personal and social relationships by their inability to communicate. Their lack of speech signals their dislocation, and Grove's.

Phil expects some acknowledgment for saving the raft-man from drowning, but he does not speak, and Phil remains silent as well: "I wished to speak, to say something. But, after having been silent so long, it seemed inconsiderate to start speaking now; there was something indelicate about my words; I gave it up" (*America* 256). Phil immediately feels an affinity for the raft-man – he notes their similarity in height and starts to imitate the man's physical actions. He also recognizes their common dislocation: "As for the peculiarities of this representative of the genus homo, I did not feel called upon to judge him. I did no longer forget that possibly my own mentality would seem abnormal to most people with whom I might come into contact" (259). This is a critical moment for Phil. He realizes that his search is not geographical and decides to return to human society; the "so long" he has been silent is the more than three months since he has encountered a human being. He is, he has told us, in the depths; he has actively avoided encounters with other people; he has almost ceased to eat; he has been drifting and lost his raft. It is his own life that has been threatened: like the raft-man, he is in danger of going down almost willingly, without a shout. After their several days and nights of silence the raft-man responds to his farewell: "And something startling happened. The man spoke. He spoke with an effort, twisting his whole body in the act, the words sounding like those of an overgrown boy when he is changing his voice, hoarse, unexpectedly loud and husky. It looked and sounded as if he were heaving the words up from, let me say, his abdomen and ejecting them forcibly. What he said was, 'I reckon'" (259). This is also a critical moment for Grove: his first words *as Grove* could not have been less laboured or dramatic. He must, by force of will, speak over and past the gulf that the denial of personality and past has caused; he must simultaneously fiction-alize his life around a constructed personality and past while sup-pressing the "true" version. In this double act he becomes his own text; Canada, as site of this discursive creativity, becomes text as well.

Phil's return to speech and society involves communication and participation, activities he has eschewed in his disillusionment. It is very likely that Grove, too, experienced a similar period of isolation and disillusionment between his disappearance from Europe in 1909 and his official arrival in Manitoba in 1912. Certainly it was a period of silence: he attempted to leave few direct traces of those years. But his eventual return to speech is inevitable, as is his obsession with his silence and with an audience for his writing.[5] The issue of audience focuses the extremity of Grove's circum-stances. The audience for his publications must also function as an audience for the reception of Frederick Philip Grove: the two transmissions are simultaneous. On one level his lack of public recognition simply underlines his personal and private anonymity and duplicity: "But who was I?" (*Myself* 7) He has no conclusive connection with a clearly identifiable and sympathetic audience: his ties with the old world are ambiguous, tortuous, and attenuated, and those with the new are non-existent. As he says himself, "A man who lives in America does not really know that there is such a thing in the world as Europe" ("Rebels All" 72). His condition is reflected in Phil Branden's, whose emigration is not by choice or design: the character of that emigration results in disorientation and isolation. Branden becomes anonymous and silent, since his European identity has no validity in his new circumstances, and he neither hears nor speaks what has been his accustomed language. Phil cannot speak across that gap; on another level, Grove must.

The construction and public reception of the Grove persona and the ongoing act of writing come together in a textual and personal construction, the autobiography *In Search of Myself*. Grove's pre-occupation with his past caused his resonant statements about the nature of identity and personal past that appeared elsewhere and earlier. An important passage occurs in "Rebels All: Of the Inter-pretation of Individual Life": "Our past, as we see it, ... does not consist in facts at all but in such fictions as have become necessary through that which followed. Yet we call it 'the past' as if it ever existed the way we see it. Thus we arrive at the paradox that, as the past influences the future, so also does the future influence the past" (74).[6] Grove's autobiography proves that statement. The text occurs within a framework he creates for its reception: the reading of the Gide biography, which forces him to face and account for his apparent failure as a writer. The pose is carefully designed to elicit both sympathy and admiration – his "failure" is to have written and published nine books as well as numerous shorter pieces in Canada in twenty-four years – within the elaborate frame-work for the text that mediates between him and what he perceives is an indifferent Canadian audience, and the European life that has made the book necessary. Of course only he knows how crucial the European life, including the European works he dare not claim, have made all this.

Revealing much more of himself than his contemporary readers could have realized, he identifies his critical problem as the absence of an audience:

What, so I asked myself, had been the reason of my thus grievously disappointing my friend, the Frenchman? There were several superficial reasons, of course. But the chief reason no doubt was that I had never had an audience; for no matter what one may say, he says it to somebody;

and if there is nobody to hear, it remains as though it had never been said; the tree falling in a forest where there is none to hear, produces no sound. A book arises as much in the mind of the reader as in that of the writer; and the writer's art consists above all in creating response; the effect of a book is the result of a collaboration between writer and audience. That collaboration I had failed to enforce ...

My struggle had been such as to make defeat a foregone conclusion. Did it matter? To whom should it matter? To me? But who was I? And suddenly it seemed to me that the only thing that really mattered was the explanation of that defeat. To whom explain it?   (6–7)

In Grove's own assessment he is facing a void. Although his pose is artificial, the necessity exercising him is not: he *has* lost the European audience, the one that matters most to him, and feels ignored by the Canadian literary community. But he needs an audience for *himself* as well as for his book: the fiction of *In Search of Myself* makes his past as he wants it to be, and perhaps his future as well, since it consolidates his position in Canadian letters. What audience and reputation he enjoys in his lifetime are never enough, however, for the man who is on the fringes in both Europe and Canada, wanting recognition, respect, and a sense of belonging: a sense of failure permeates the work. He cannot go back to the place he actually came from or to the one he imagines, but he can and does direct his art there. He constructs self, place, and audience:

The lack of an audience? But even the lack of an audience is not the important thing. The important thing is that *you* have such an audience *in mind* when you speak. Whether it is really there does not matter. In case of need you can imagine it. But was there any need for me to imagine it? If I could explain, to someone, why I had failed, the explanation might more than compensate for the failure to have made myself heard so far. Could I explain it? I did not know. I saw the reasons clearly enough. I must try. And "to someone"? To whom? To whom but my friend the young Frenchman who was now a man of seventy or more? Whether he ever read the explanation, what did it matter?   (10–11)

Gide as audience is absent and their friendship another of Grove's inventions,[7] but he functions fictionally and rhetorically: thus Grove is not speaking simply out of one void into another but within a placed discursive relation. Facing Europe, his writing becomes addressed and transmissible and is ensured a response from his Canadian audience, which will, as it were, overhear.

The autobiography, as a conclusion to the elaborate hoax and a measure of its success, occurs near the end of Grove's life, as his actions and the years prove just how irreversible his break with the old world is and as he becomes more and more obsessed with what he has left behind. At the end it is apparent that whatever degree of coherence of self he has achieved, he has not achieved a coherence of place: although he may at times have Fred Grove more or less in place, his placing of Canada is tentative and hypothetical. The concentration required to create the self and put it into action in the absence of the accustomed structures or understandings limits his ability, energy, and desire to direct the same degree of concentration and insight at the new world. The Canada he creates necessarily exhibits gaps and absences that, with his personal history and cultural and discursive displacement, he simply cannot fill. He is less able to create a sense of Canada than of Europe partly because he knows the new setting less well, but largely because he can infuse it with less of himself: in Europe he was an intact, coherent person, but in Canada he must struggle to maintain presence. Canada is, correspondingly, similarly threatened because of the interdependent relationship Grove has created in his search for the new world and himself.

Grove dreams Europe if only to find a place to be from (Kroetsch "Finding"). He no less dreams North America as he searches for his ideal across the continent. His creation of Canada is physical and cartographic: this is literally the possession and inhabitation of the new world, the transformation of space to place. But Grove's empirical acts of surveying and settling occur in his texts, within the imaginative, metaphorical processes of language: the inhabitation of the new world is discursive. The inhabitation of the new world is also ontological and existential, with the attending anxiety and distortion that show in Grove's work as he writes himself and the landscape into existence: he writes of "the bush-country of Manitoba as I had 'created' it; for the landscape as it lives in this novel and in others, and its human inhabitants as well, were mine, were the product of my mind" (*Myself* 373). In claiming ownership, he insists on that world's insubstantiality. There are insufficiencies in that created landscape and in his ability to create it: he is only partially sustained by that structure because of its nature and his own, and the distance his past puts between himself and his present place. He wants and needs it to be as secure for him as the old world was, but that is not possible. Part of Grove's difficulty in the relationship between self and place is the discrepancy between the actual and the imagined environment. His Canada is imagined just as his identity and his Europe is, and he is bound to be disappointed when reality does not fit with the imagined version: Canada is as he wants it to be only in his fiction, where he can move the roads and place the farmsteads, and where the landscape and its inhabitants "had become more real than any actuality could have been" (*Myself* 373).

The fiction he created about himself claimed him in the way his heroes' creations claimed them, and was a more valid spiritual history than his own experience had been. His autobiographical act is doubly metaphoric: the act, and the texts it produces, constitute not a self but a metaphor of self.[8] Grove's may be a classic act of autobiography, if autobiographical truth is not a fixed but an evolving content in an intricate process of self-discovery and self-creation, and if the self that is the centre of all autobiographical narrative is a fictive structure. The complex fictive structure of Grove's identity and life is an illustration of the interdependence of self and language. Grove writes himself into existence as a social being and as an individual. He has to create and maintain a closed world for himself: if he allows the infinite to intrude, the consequences will be unlimited and uncontrollable. Grove's and his pioneers' environments are created and controlled by his imagination: he writes himself as he writes the pioneers on to the prairie he has created for them and himself. His physical descriptions of human settlements and journeys or human actions in nature become cartographers' instructions as he charts human progress in classificatory systems of distance and direction. The inscription of the survey grid is a mark of human definition, critical to the pioneer and to Grove, although that order of farmyards and fences is, again, Grove's own: "But although I have not consciously introduced any changes in the landscape as God made it, I have in fairness to the settlers entirely redrawn the superimposed man-made landscape" (*Trails* 8n). The map must be redrawn, the world remade, not to protect the settlers but to create the image of human order on the natural landscape and to secure human identity and existence. If not, if the landscape remains unmarked not only by human order but by his own order, human existence for Grove is negated. The new world, as setting and material, both requires and allows this activity; always on the edge of disintegration, it is the only place Grove can exist at all.

The order the pioneer creates in the landscape is his defence, as Grove's writing is his. Grove is not simply the subject of his own writing – his life *is* his narrative. If to write history and autobiography is to perform metaphorically a work of personal restoration and to reintegrate the self in culture, a process not unlike the reintegration that may follow the liminal phase, and further, if to write is to constitute reality, then the moment of language originates not only the self but its social reality as well. In this frame Grove's autobiographical acts are fully consistent and comprehensible, and are necessarily registers of new world discourse as well. The temptation of the universal and the transcendental in the remaking of FPG that Healy finds reminiscent of Whitman (96) identifies the register in which Grove's activity and, accordingly, new world discourse in Canada occurs. The significance of his origination of self as he acquires language is doubled by his use of English for his Canadian writing. If the history of the self is coextensive with discourse itself, it is significant that when Greve becomes Grove his status as a German speaker is rendered uncertain. Without the repeated assertion of control, order, and meaning that he can exert in his writing, now in English, the alternative of his own non-meaning – the suicide he faked – threatens. If he loses *this* language he will disappear for what is for him the second time. He cannot risk that personal and cultural dislocation again. The constructed persona in Canada, created by will and whim, would be even easier to erase than his Greve existence. He is intent on making a closed and secure place for himself in Canada: the covered cutter he uses for his journeys between Gladstone and Falmouth speaks of his need for protection as he crosses a blank space in which he can be lost and obliterated. His civil and colonial space remain radically in question.

Like his settlers', Grove's identity is dependent on his creation. While the pioneers define themselves with fences and farmyards and names of districts, Grove spends his life in North America attempting to put himself into a discourse, declaring both his lack of language (*Myself* 338) and his personal absence: "I believe I have hidden myself fairly well" (*Myself* 383). His silences are about

himself and his past, and within the characters in his novels. In the
second chapter of *A Search for America* he uses both the first and
third persons, describing to his readers "the young man that was I"
(21) and showing that young man desperately attempting to retain
his sense of himself as a dignified European. Phil can barely communicate with North Americans, and the lack of his accustomed
discourse eventually results in the silent withdrawal and isolation
of "The Depths." Neither Phil nor Grove can fully enter the
discourse of the new world. The same gap in understanding that
would prevent Grove from using that discourse for his desired
European audience prevents him from entering it himself.

Grove's invented world holds, with constant reinforcement. It
does not enable him to move beyond character types in his portrayal of male pioneers, but it does provide him with one of his
subjects, the chronicle of life on the prairies, which fulfils his need
to build structures that give meaning to himself and to North
America: fence-posts and families, cartography and community. He
has little knowledge of the personal attributes of individual North
Americans, and when he attempts to put an individual into society
he produces the pioneer novels, such as *Settlers of the Marsh*, *Fruits
of the Earth*, and *Our Daily Bread*, in which the personal emotional
relationships are awkward and wrong. Even so, this human relatedness is critical, since it has the power either to reinforce or to
destroy individual identity in this dubious universe. The problematic nature of human relationships is not resolved in the Canadian
works[9] and is expressed in Grove's portrayal of character. His
Canadian novels are largely about patriarchs, to whom he cannot
extend even a fictional flexibility, while the women are marginal;
in his German novels the women are the protagonists. His new
world identity and personality are rigidly defined, and necessarily
so: the question of identity for him in the new world is personal,
and male. A condition of personal relatedness and connectedness
that was intact for Greve in Europe is not so for Grove in Canada,
and the old and new world discourses differ accordingly.

In "F.P. Grove: The Finding," Robert Kroetsch expresses Grove's
need to construct his world in terms of family relationships:

> we say with your waiting wife   (but she
> was the world   before you invented it
> old liar)   "You had a hard trip?" (47)

The same need operates in the characters in his novels. Like John Elliot in the ontological meditation *Our Daily Bread*, the discrepancies between Grove's public record and his private life are enormous, and there are many things he cannot speak of directly. But much is said indirectly. The tricks in the autobiographies – the hints at his past and the tantalizingly partial truths[10] – and the wry humour he can occasionally afford show the intense pressure he feels to keep his reality intact and under control. In the prairie novels the incomplete and fragmented natures of personalities like Elliot's is most clearly apparent within the family. John Elliot's ambition is to realize himself as an Old Testament patriarch, scattering his children fruitfully on the land around him: his life takes meaning and purpose from that vision. His sense of himself as patriarch depends on his children being extensions of himself, or at most "a compound of the two parent natures" (10), but when those personalities are totally their own, his conception of himself is destroyed. Elliot's self-creation is a failure because he has located its source externally; ironically, his children fail too, because they are determined to repudiate their father's example and ideals. His wife's rejection of him, tellingly an early symptom of her eventual madness, are the manifestations of her protest at his attempt to create himself out of her. The artifacts of Grove's and Elliot's lives both prove their existence and negate their humanity. Elliot does not possess the identity he spent his life trying to assemble, nor the ability to speak of his goal; he dies in the wreck of his house, a legend whose pioneer "story [is] an inspiration" (183) but whose personal life is a failure.[11] Grove's record is similarly ambivalent.

In *Our Daily Bread* Elliot is unable to move into a close and honest relationship with his family, although it is clear in the text that both he and Grove know that this is what could transform his family into a meaningful version of the dynasty he is determined to create. In *Settlers of the Marsh* Niels' redemption, although incomplete, is his marriage with Ellen, which functions as a symbol for his reconnection to a human world of emotion, commitment, and responsibility. Sam Clark in *The Master of the Mill* is aware that had he married the right woman, his life would have been much different. Abe is determined to leave his name and mark on the district in *Fruits of the Earth*, but his reconciliation with his family fails. These men are all outsiders, like the detached observer in *Over Prairie Trails* and Grove himself. The relationships in

Greve's German novels do not carry the same pressure: although the problematic nature of relationships between women and men forms the basis of the plots of *The Master Mason's House* and *Fanny Essler*, neither the world nor the protagonists crumble because they are not happy in love. Greve has little at stake in these novels, drawing on a life that is not yet problematic.[12] The protagonists of Greve's German works are women who are strong enough to make decisions and to act, although their successes are qualified. Grove's Canadian women are silent and largely absent, functioning as figures who act as a revolving background and foreground for the men rather than as strong intact people.[13] They are closer than their husbands to a coherent sense of self within harmonious human relationships, although those relationships are more often with their children, but we do not see enough of them: although Grove says his sympathies are with the women (*Myself* 224), in the Canadian novels his attention is not.

Because he is interested in more than an image of a human being in society, Grove cannot limit his writing to fiction. He cannot avoid his intense preoccupation with himself in private and public roles – thus the mixture of genres in the two *Searches*.[14] By insisting on his identity as a writer, he shows the imperative he felt to make himself not only visible but highly and publicly so in his new life: his dislocation insists that it be declared in writing and in an order that is more than simply personal. Asserting himself as a writer became a shorthand and coded way for Grove to assert his sense of self, which was part of his imperative for survival after his flight from Germany (Healy 90). Grove is under perpetual threat: as Spettigue puts it, "art and the artist give form and meaning to existence, and existence reasserts its formlessness and meaninglessness to deny them" ("Fanny Essler" 62–3). The primary act of declaring oneself has to take place in language as well as in life; as Grove himself realized, "my life was, or should have been, the life of the imagination" (*Myself* 452). In a very real sense, his Canadian life was.

Grove's inhabitation of the new world and its discourse is not an unqualified success, but it is remarkable that he managed it at all. He is not able to complete the portrait of the socialized individual in his own life: his story in Canada is littered with confrontations with school-boards and resignations from teaching positions. He admits his temptation to go to the wall, but settles for what he calls the wilderness (Pacey *Letters* 13). There is, accordingly, a distance between himself and his own self-portraits in the autobiographical works and the characters in his fiction. His works are starred with the recognitions of what is necessary for himself and his characters to move beyond generalized, sociological inquiries, but he is unable to show a coherent, intact, and placed identity. Grove may say that he takes root in western Canada, but he survives rather than flourishes. Something is missing in the transaction: he simply cannot reconnect in a vital way, although he goes through all the right motions – family, profession, property – to do so. He must have more than simply a sociological model to make the social place and the connections of kinship. Working within a new language, a new place, and a new existence, he tries to create himself out of an experience he must not acknowledge. To do that he must also create the new place and a way to speak of it. Grove remains essentially, in his Canadian existence, an inarticulate man. His life was the imaginative masterpiece he kept trying to write.

Both Grove's life and writing constitute new world discourse because of the unique circumstances of his life. That integral relation between personal, literary, and cultural constructions in Grove's case echoes Richardson's to some extent, and says something important about the metaphoric processes through which a cultural place comes to exist. There is little sense in either Richardson's or Grove's work of cultural sanction; rather, there is a profound sense of exhaustion. Grove's possession and inhabitation of the new world is a precise and definitive example of the way in which the namer's point of view conditions the acts of seeing and writing the new world: for Grove the point of view is absolutely determined by his old world frame of reference and his removal to the new world, rather than by new world experience itself. In choosing western Canada for the initial adaptation to his new world life, Grove parallels the pattern of Canada's physical exploration and settlement; again, discursive and cultural practices are integrally related. As Frederick Philip Grove comes into existence in the new world, the new world does as well. Grove's world is dependent on his existence there; that existence is made possible and sustained in the metaphoric process of language. Grove invents the new world as he invents himself: both entities have meaning only as Grove's need causes them and his imagination creates them.

The inconsistencies and gaps in his writing reveal the extreme pressures inherent in naming and inhabiting the Grove persona and the conceptual place, as well as their tentative and essential attachment to each other. His sense of the provisional nature of Canada, which he expressed in his first speaking tour, remains ("Canadians Old and New" 171). Grove lives the new world's discursive invention; his writing both invests new world discourse with meaning and takes its own meaning from that condition.

CHAPTER FOUR

Sheila Watson:
On Soft Ground

The Double Hook shows how the questions of Canada and human being in Canada are framed by and within new world discourse. In *The Double Hook* we do not see the uneasy and unsuccessful coexistence of old world forms of thought and writing with new world setting and experience, as is the case with both Richardson and Grove. Rather, in her novel Sheila Watson enacts the construction of new world discourse while articulating the risks surrounding the process. She fragments the intertexts of Western culture to show that meaning and human being are possible only within discursive structures; she thematizes this issue by having figures move from speech to silence to speech again, an event that resonates with echoes of classical, Christian, and native mythologies of creation and apocalypse. The danger in moving into silence is one that Watson and the novel share: such a radical questioning of the possibility of human language implicates human being and human culture as well.

Watson avoids the psychic and cultural non-existence in which such a process could logically and easily end by maintaining the text on two levels. On one level the five-part comedic narrative allows James's flight and return to result in increased self-knowledge and a reconciliation with his child's mother, which in turn renews the entire community and retrieves it from its previous violence and insensibility. On another level, the terror provoked by the act of matricide that initiates the novel's action calls up the new world's conditions of dissociation, loss, and nightmare, with the attendant imperative to transform the new space into a discursive place.[1] The gap between discursive universes is the gap between old and new world discourses, and exists within the text as the silence into which the novel's figures, readers, and the new world itself may fall. The closure Watson imposes on the narrative level is echoed by transformations on the metaphorical level that allow language to reclaim meaning and the new world to claim and sustain itself fully. The new world takes up its hybrid condition, positioned precisely between certainty and enigma.

For Watson the movement from old to new world discursive universes constitutes an interrogation of language. *The Double Hook* addresses directly the new world phenomenon and the break from Europe, the loss in the transferral from the old world, and the essential discontinuity between the lives lived in that place and those lived in other places. It shows too the loss of the established, placed social structure – the world-in-itself phenomenon – and how the images of the world that language provided simply by being in that other place do not register or function in the new world. The loss of history, memory, belonging, and language is disorienting and disabling for the indigenous culture, which has suffered from the European refusal to acknowledge its existence and validity, as well as for the immigrating culture.[2] Watson speaks to this point: "I was concerned too, in another sort of way I suppose, with the problem of an indigenous population which had lost or was losing its own mythic structure, which had had its images destroyed, its myths interpreted for it by various missionary societies and later by anthropologists – a group intermarried or intermingled with people of other beliefs – French Catholics who had come into the West with the Hudson Bay Company, Biblical puritanical elements – all now virtually isolated from their source" (Meyer and O'Riordan 159). The dynamic resulting from these multiple fragment cultures joining with the indigenous element – which, paradoxically, has become a fragment in its own place – defines new world discourse and causes *The Double Hook*.

The novel is informed by an awareness of the complicated procedures on many levels that a new society in a new place must negotiate in order to make some meaning of itself, as well as by Watson's aesthetic sense and her grounding in modernism.[3] Her awareness of culture registers discursively: it shows in the collapse into silence and invisibility that the figures in this novel so completely enact. Their liminal existence and the extreme disruption of their patterns of myth, kinship, and language show not only the excessive degree of consciousness that these structures demand in these circumstances but also the extreme pressure motivating Watson's creation of new world discourse. In the old world these structures retain content; in the new there is only the imperative that they be re-created. The new world culture exists only in so far as it can take possession of itself and its place metaphorically, in language. In so doing it reforms the compact between language and meaning and assembles a social and historical frame, thereby gaining visibility in a landscape and place that deny its existence.

In *The Double Hook* Watson refuses to posit Canada as a secure social structure with eternity in place. One is thrown back to origin, and the origin is literally the Word, with the old lady's act of inscription on the baked mud of the lake bottom. But Watson undercuts this informing act immediately: there is no assured salvation in this word, no guarantee of transformation. The interdependent association of language and meaning that she insists on is double-hooked: if the presence of language gives meaning to people and place, its absence withdraws that meaning, totally. Watson suggests that if the meaning of a sentence disappears, the meaning of human being will as well, and the meaning of sentences is often uncertain in this novel: "In the sky above evil had gathered strength. It took body writhing and twisting under the high arch. Lenchen could hear the breath of it in the pause. The swift indrawing. The silence of the contracting muscle. The head drop for the wild plunge and hoof beat of it" (41). Experience and reality have to be *made* meaningful, to be mediated and translated in language, but in the peculiar conditions of the new world they may instead be lost if a discourse in which they would register is not present or accessible – a double hook indeed. That hook is the novel's and Watson's own: it is also the new world's.

It is precisely Watson's doubled focus – both on the theoretical and philosophical bases of new world discourse and culture and on the processes that fragment and reassemble modes of speaking and human existence – that makes new world discourse both the subject and form of the novel. Watson repeatedly cancels the meaning of words and disappoints the expectation that language will resolve the tensions and conflicts brought about by the text, while hinting that such indeterminacies will be resolved only when we understand our ways of knowing in this place. As Judith Miller aptly puts it, Watson leaves unexplained gaps for us to be in alone, and trusts

silences that are full of the echoes from the words around them
(220). The intertextual nature of the work, which relies on the code
texts of the books of the Prophets, the Psalms, Roman Catholic
liturgy, native mythology, classical mythology, and modernist literature, requires the reader to listen to the echoes, close the gaps, and
make the connections that Watson refuses to, at least at one level.
At the beginning of the novel these connections are absent at the
level of syntax, and the reader is forced to fill in the missing subjects
of sentences: "James walking away. The old lady falling. There
under the jaw of the roof. In the vault of the bed loft. Into the
shadow of death. Pushed by James's will. By James's hand. By
James's words: This is my day. You'll not fish today" (19). The
reader must also recognize the intertext itself to realize the weight
of significance Watson has put on her discursive dismantling:

His mind sifted ritual phrases. Some half forgotten. You're welcome. Put
your horse in. Pull up. *Ave Maria. Benedictus fructus ventris. Introibo.*

Introibo. The beginning. The whole thing to live again. Words said over
and over here by the stove. His father knowing them by heart. God's
servants. The priest's servants. The cup lifting. The bread breaking.
Domine non sum dignus. Words coming. The last words.

He rolled from his chair. Stood barefoot. His hands raised.

Pax vobiscum, he said.

The girl lifted her head. She licked the saliva from the corner of her mouth.

What the hell, she said.

Go in peace, he said.   (51)

Throughout the text Watson repeatedly uses indefinite pronouns,
incomplete sentences, and repetition (Godard 158–9), dislocates
sentence structure, contrasts her diction with conventional usage,
obscures events of plot, and extends the distance between word
and meaning until the link, if it remains at all, is fragile and
tenuous. Watson's words suggest that what she intends is something
that transcends the literal meaning of words and physical phenomena: "He went out of the kitchen into the sun. Outside the world
floated like a mote in a straight shaft of glory. A horse coming
round the corner of the barn shone copper against the hewn logs,
Kip riding black on its reflected brightness" (26). Although she
privileges Western culture with her choice of intertexts, her suggestion of infinite possibilities makes us recognize that those texts no

longer contain the world. Her determination to stretch and break
the connection between language and referent makes her linguistic
practice teeter in the gap between old and new world discourse.
The world – the word – floats, rather like Greta's fixed and
uncertain pump (22). Watson also makes clear that we are dealing
with literature, with sets of associations and stories, not with a
"realistic" story of life in contemporary British Columbia (Miller
214): we might well take seriously Arnold Davidson's warning
about being caught on the hook of story (40). The result of
Watson's discursive methods is that both the literary and cultural
levels are deliberately put into question within the text.

The position that both the text and the reader assume between
the dismantling of one discursive construction and the formation
of another results in the threat of annihilation at the levels of text,
person, and culture. Watson registers this threat in the discursive
practices registered within the text: words no longer mean, because
they could mean anything. The movement is towards silence or the
meaningless sound in which the entire community is trapped with
the Widow, who calls on God while denying communication and
contact: "Dear God, she cried. Then she stopped short. Afraid that
he might come" (55). William gives "half a dozen reasons for
anything" (20–1) and disallows meaning entirely by his assertion
that "thread has a hundred uses. When it comes down to it, he'd
say, there's no telling what thread is for" (21). Kip, the messenger,
either loses words or refuses to deliver them without something to
"oil up a man's mind" (62). Ara sees much but says little; James
and Greta use words to drive Lenchen away. There are no fixed
limits or relationships of words and meaning: words do not explain
or even describe the old lady's activity as she lights her lamp at
noon and fishes upstream to the source. The same words – "She's
here" – refer to three sightings, in three settings, all while she is
lying dead in her bed. The movement towards silence and meaningless sound is enacted not only by the figures in the text: even
the landscape is "noisy and restless in its silence" (53).

Much of the power of *The Double Hook* and the questions of
structure and language that arise from it are related to landscape
and to Watson's attention to the conceptualization of this place.
The natural environment is an unformed and threatening absence
and chaos. Watson's description of the setting makes the valley –
and the new world – a peculiarly insubstantial place, in which

reality is impossible to define or know. Stephen Scobie characterizes the description astutely: "We are given not so much a landscape as the *signs* of a landscape, not so much description as the semiotic conventions of description reduced to their most basic forms" (*Sheila Watson* 19). Darkness is literally upon the face of the deep: "Still the old lady fished. If the reeds had dried up and the banks folded and crumbled down she would have fished still. If God had come into the valley, come holding out the long finger of salvation, moaning in the darkness, thundering down the gap at the lake head, skimming across the water, drying up the blue signature like blotting-paper, asking where, asking why, defying an answer, she would have thrown her line against the rebuke; she would have caught a piece of mud and looked it over; she would have drawn a line with the barb when the fire of righteousness baked the bottom" (20). The old lady dragging her hook across the baked mud bed of the lake is enacting creation, but through the metaphoric and imaginative processes of language: only in these terms can this world be created and exist. Her act of creation takes the form of inscription, with its echo of speech: "Let there be light" both undercuts and resonates behind this passage. That kind of resonance, occurring here and repeatedly throughout the text, builds tension and piles up suggestions of both genesis and apocalypse.

It is on this metaphoric plane that Watson sees the possibility of the new world's existence; if the metaphoric nature of the text's language is not recognized, roads will continue to run from this to that, hills fall off to nowhere (33), and water rise in drought to kill (21). She shows that in these conditions place is informed by absurdity, human being floats, and both figures and ground are ready to unravel into abstraction: "If a man lost the road in the land round William Potter's, he couldn't find his way by keeping to the creek bottom for the creek flowed this way and that at the land's whim. The earth fell away in hills and clefts as if it had been dropped carelessly wrinkled on the bare floor of the world" (22). As the old lady's invocation of genesis and apocalypse is not heard, this landscape is perceived to be not intelligible and created but absurd and random – formless and "floorless, roofless, wall-less" (66) – in which physical phenomena cannot be accounted for: "The most unaccountable thing, [William]'d say, is the way the sun falls. I've seen a great cow, he'd say, throw no more shadow for its calf than a lean rabbit" (22). There is little possibility that such a landscape will allow or sustain human existence: "There are men, [William]'d say, have seen their whole place fade like a cheap shirt. And there's no way a man can fold it up and bring it in out of the sun. You can save a cabbage plant or a tomato plant with tents of paper if you've got the paper, but there's no human being living can tent a field and pasture" (21). The entire valley becomes as insubstantial as those tents of paper, or the hills "pegged like tanned skin to the rack of their own bones" (127). The "flat ribs of the hills" (35) and "the raw skin of the sky" (36) defy the categorization of natural phenomena and deny the boundaries between humans, animals, and the elements. Physical human existence is at risk in this landscape: James fears "dying somewhere alone, caught against a tree or knocked over in an inch of water" (42). Watson suggests the metaphysical context of such a death by evoking crucifixion, but that context is not recognized or articulated in this community; accordingly, James's fear appears to be irrational and unprovoked and is all the more paralysing.

The landscape's temptation to absurdity and randomness is underlined in the equivocal account Watson provides of its source. The native trickster gives the landscape its ambivalent meaning – "Coyote made the land his pastime. He stretched out his paw. He breathed on the grass. His spittle eyed it with prickly pear" (22) – and his voice haunts the imagination: "Above on the hills / Coyote's voice rose among the rocks: / In my mouth is forgetting / In my darkness is rest" (29). Watson, however, will not make him absolute. Ara blends God and Coyote in an image of power and cruelty – "The glory of his face shaded by his hat. Not coaxing with pans of oats, but coming after you with a whip until you stand and face him in the end" (77) – in her conviction that the biblical God has no bearing on this place or these lives: "Even God's eye could not spy out the men lost here already, Ara thought. He had looked mercifully on the people of Nineveh though they did not know their right hand and their left. But there were not enough people here to attract his attention. The cattle were scrub cattle. The men lay like sift in the cracks of the earth" (22–3). Jehovah is real to the Widow, however, as is the dread of punishment at Judgment. The biblical God exists as well in the patterns of Coyote's speech, which are formed on the books of the Prophets as well as on the Psalms and the Mass. By undercutting both registers as she introduces them, Watson disallows a secure position for either the figures in her novel or its readers: this condition of the text comes near to undoing the reader, as well as the text and the issues it has raised. As the reader is implicated in these complicated transitions between existence and annihilation, the world Watson undercuts is one's own: there is no circular completion here, but a flat disc that threatens to tip and slide one off its edge to nowhere.

There is no immunity from this metaphysical insecurity within the text, nor from Coyote and his powerful temptation of darkness and oblivion: "Coyote reaching out reflected glory. Like a fire to warm. Then shoving the brand between a man's teeth right into his belly's pit. Fear making mischief. Laying traps for men. The dog and his servants plaguing the earth" (61). The plague that Coyote and his servants have laid upon nature and humanity is, necessarily, discursive. The figures in the novel live "suspended in silence. When they spoke they spoke of hammers and buckles, of water for washing, of rotted posts, of ringbone and distemper" (43). Speech in any register other than the mundane and concrete has stopped. The sense of the metaphorical is inaccessible; the sense of loss is acute. Felix's speech defines one aspect of that loss, but his mixture of fragments of the Mass with "scatter" and "get-the-hell-out" brings him quickly to the end of his saying (51). He and his neighbours are not a community and cannot be made so, or even be nailed together like boards (86) – they exist without perception or meaningful speech in a condition of violence and insensibility. Their cultural and linguistic practices have become as arbitrary and insubstantial as the landscape: they have accordingly lost their protection against the threat of non-meaning. They are threatened with annihilation in this space where words mean nothing because they do not mean more than they say.

Watson believes that words mean and that the limits of language are the limits of the world: "I don't think words are innocent. Sometimes the impact of words on a reader is not what the writer expects at all ... Words are not simple exchange. They are charged. They have all sorts of possibilities which may explode at any moment ... literature is not innocent because it has the power to produce a disequilibrium in your life ... a violation, a transgression of sensibility ... man is freed from his animal condition but he is freed into a more perilous condition through language" (Meyer and O'Riordan 162–3). That more perilous condition is, in the new world, doubly charged. Existing only discursively, the new world's freedom is in one sense absolute; its existence, then, is both conditional upon and made fragile by that freedom. In these circumstances Watson is clear to articulate the responsibility that accompanies language. In this text words can kill: the old lady is "pushed ... by James's words" (19). Of course Watson's point is that words can speak this world, as well as a person, in or out of existence. The threat of that power and its possible misuse is coded throughout the text. When James returns from the town below he has been freed from the freedom he gained when he tried to escape from his mother, Lenchen, and Coyote. His new condition has an increased potential both for new life and its denial: riding into the first pasture of things with plans for his new home, he may well be starting the whole cycle of self-destruction all over again, with memory held like a knife in his hand, clasped shut (127). Neither is it clear that Coyote has released him. As William, Heinrich, and Ara wait for James at the smoking ruins of his house, they hear a voice in the hills: "Above them a coyote barked. This time they could see it on a jut of rock calling down over the ledge so that the walls of the valley magnified its voice and sent it echoing back: Happy are the dead for their eyes see no more" (114–15). The ambivalence caused by "a coyote" rather than "Coyote" and by the words that suggest that insensibility is preferable to intelligent existence is reinforced by Coyote's blessing on Lenchen's Felix, which closes the book: "I have set his feet on soft ground; / I have set his feet on the sloping shoulders of the world" (134). The new world is secured only in language; its inhabitation can only be imaginative and metaphoric.

The alternative is the risk that attends discursive practice without referent, the risk in the extended moment between the acknowledgment of the dysfunction of the discursive structures of the old world discourse and the full and complete possession of the new. As it becomes meaningless sound, language is no longer the domain of the human or a register of human existence – note Watson's talking parrot and coyote. The result of the inquiry that Watson initiates here is intense epistemological questioning: her investigation of the relationship between language and the world, the way of knowing as well as what is known, results in profound ambivalence. Neither of Coyote's registers, the Scriptures from which the patterns of his speech come nor the trickster legend from which he comes, is enabling in this context. Watson wants to make his speaking equivocal in its promises of revelation and annihilation, and threatening in its suggestion that the silent gap between old and new worlds is permanent and unbridgeable. The parrot's rote repetition of language, as effective as the townspeople's speech, makes the same point: "The parrot swung itself below the inside edge of the counter and came up with a tin mug in one claw. 'Drinks on you,' it said ... James looked up. The parrot seemed to be watching him over the rim of its mug. 'She was old,' James said, speaking to the parrot" (100–1). The usurpation of a human faculty by an animal threatens to undo the structure and meaning of the world: if human beings allow the perilous freedom of their language to be diminished in this way, they will be unable to construct or inhabit any discursive formation. A full and authoritative inhabitation of the new world is put radically into question, as is the possibility of human being itself. The new world cannot exist in the negation of human discourse.

The crisis that the text presents is forestalled on its narrative level by a re-linking of human community and human speaking, and thematic closure. Heinrich's initial silence – "How could he say that the earth scorched his foot. That he must become ash and be born into a light which burned but did not destroy" (81) – is replaced by his recognition of personal responsibility and human community: "Can a man speak to no one because he's a man? Who says so? Those who want to be sheltered by his silence. I've held my tongue, he said, when I should have used my voice like an axe to cut down the wall between us" (82). Similarly, Felix's blessed peace, which has threatened to become the silence of the damned, is broken when he goes for Angel to help him with Lenchen and Kip: "All the way up the road he'd been trying to form the words" (78). The words are the translated "Peace be with you" and "Angel, ... I need you" (78, 79). James turns his back on silence and meaningless speech after speaking to the parrot about his mother's death. He knows that he must publicly acknowledge his guilt and responsibility by speaking: his first words on his return are "Lenchen ... I left her here" (131). He also knows that his return has been inevitable: "James turned to the boy. What could he say of the light that had made him want to drink fire into his darkness. Of the child got between the leafless trees when the frost was stiff in the branches. Of beating up Kip and running off because Kip had been playing round with the glory of the world. I ran away, he said, but

I circled and ended here the way a man does when he's lost" (132). The child embodies a genuine and positive rebirth; by enacting together the rituals of burial and birth, the community is renewed.

The crisis must also be forestalled on the text's other level. For this to occur, Watson has to transform this space of nothingness and absence, with as much significance as an apron dropped wrinkled like the earth on the bare floor of the world, to a meaningful place filled with a powerful presence where reduction on all levels is no longer demanded: "There's no big Coyote, like you think. There's not just one of him. He's everywhere. The government's got his number too. They've set a bounty on him at fifty cents a brush" (57). In this passage Watson articulates the new world dilemma. Naming invents the new world. In naming coyote rather than Coyote, Theophil shows that he does not inhabit the new world of imagination and metaphor. His life will continue to be one of isolation and terminal insensibility (Scobie *Sheila Watson* 25), with fear growing like fur over his eyes (58). The others in the text as well, except possibly Felix, fear what we understand to be the transformation into new world discourse, although Theophil is alone in refusing it. Human speech is gradually redeemed from its reliance on meaningless cliché and vague, intangible "things"; even the Widow's lamentations come to be directed outward, signalling determination and action rather than despair: "Dear God, said the Widow, it's a feeble cry. Quick. Quick, she called and clambered down from the box as Ara pulled the horses to a stop before the door ... The Widow's hand was on the knob ... Dear God, she said, the latch needs oil" (130).

This is a transitional step, preparing for the point at which Watson makes the two levels of the text intersect: the birth of Lenchen's child registers crucially in two senses. It is within the enabling context of human birth that Felix is physically and spiritually transformed, with a powerful evocation of mystery, divinity, and transcendence: "If he could only shed his flesh, moult and feather again, he might begin once more. His eyelids dropped. His flesh melted. He rose from the bed on soft owl wings. And below he saw his old body crouched down like an ox by the manger" (126). This moment is the invention of the new world. Felix becomes other, and becomes a child bearing his name: the world is transformed as well, and now exists at the level of language and imagination. This movement into metaphor is movement into new world discourse, in which a complete inhabitation of this place is now possible. Only in this transformation by imagination that Felix undergoes can space become place, something other than a meaningless and formless threat that defies human order and being.

The full and authoritative possession of its own place signals the new world's creation; the imaginative, metaphorical act constructs the discursive universe in which the new world exists. When metaphoric meaning is present and articulated, a foolhen becomes a phoenix: the environment achieves meaning by being placed in a discursive framework. This is a dramatic act in the novel, and in Canadian writing. Now Felix will fish for the people in his house as well as for the glory. Kip's physical blinding may make him more aware of the context in which he has access to the glory: his reply to Felix's question about how he'll make his living – "There's no telling at all ... There's no way of telling what will walk into a man's hand" (133) – suggests a new recognition of possibility. At the end of the novel both characters' matter-of-fact acceptance of the changed facts of their individual and community relatedness underscores the duality that the text is based on, as do Lenchen's and Ara's visions:

From the next room came the sound of the Widow's voice and the sound of Angel's hand upon the stove.

Suddenly the girl sat up.

The door's opening, she said. I see James in his plaid shirt. He's lifting the baby in his two hands.

Ara stood up. The girl wasn't speaking to her any longer; she was speaking to James.

His name is Felix, she said.

Ara didn't want to look at James. She went to the window and leaned out across the bush where the sparrow chattered. Above her the sky stretched like a tent pegged to the broken rock. And from a cleft of the rock she heard the voice of Coyote crying down through the boulders ...   (134)

As Lenchen calls her sensing of James seeing, and Ara simultaneously hears a sparrow's chatter and Coyote's voice, Watson's point is made. The metaphoric maintains the quotidian; the world is secured, ambivalently, by human imagination. Watson shows the power of the transformation in the text without allowing us to forget the threat of its very possible failure: she ends the novel with

Coyote's voice placing both the child's feet and our own on soft ground.

The Double Hook begins as an investigation not only of how to make sense of writing but of how writing makes sense of the world, a fundamental question in the new world and an epistemological inquiry at a second remove. Watson is most interested in the moral and philosophical results of this condition of silence, insensibility, and invisibility in the absence of new world discourse, and signals one possibility by placing intelligible speech in the mouth of a parrot. The other possibility is shown in the transformation of Felix. The questions the text raises are not answered by the formal and thematic closure that the narrative enacts: the tension between that closure and the registers she strikes on the text's other level is the new world's condition. As the narrative coexists with the theoretical concerns of the text, Watson allows moral and philosophical ambiguities to remain. She leaves her figures, and readers, somewhere between the indigenous myths that people the hills with the trickster and the Christian tradition that provides both an avenging Old Testament Jehovah and the poetry of the Psalms – in the neither/nor conditions of the second world. Watson is on both sides in her determination to play and to privilege language. She insists on fixing meaning and relation and on constructing the world of something real while simultaneously exploding perceptions of place and objects. She shows the possibility, necessity, and method of unravelling the discursive formation imposed upon the new world, but refuses to reduce the proposition to nothing – she is determined to reclaim meaning within those terms rather than make inevitable the final and fatal ending that attends the gap between worlds.

This new genesis is less certain in one of her short texts, "And the Four Animals." The watcher, who is also the landscape and the eye, both focuses the four ebony dogs into being and destroys them by feeding their parts to each other until they are reduced to a single tooth, which he hides in his own belly. The watcher may be a god who will re-enact creation by divine force, or a human who will re-enact creation by human imagination; the other strong possibility is a final ending.[4] This may be the conclusion Watson did not want to reach in *The Double Hook*. The difference between the endings of the two texts points up with some clarity the conflict between the contradictory pressures in the new world. In *The*

Double Hook Watson is determined to avoid the apocalyptic ending that is possible in this liminal moment between old and new world discourse. Her awareness of the conditions of the new world do not allow the novel to be a neutral or uninterested investigation of the possibility of human language and human being: her conviction that language means (Meyer and O'Riordan 166) and that it is integrally involved in the construction of a new culture brings her to this point. *Deep Hollow Creek*, written before but published after *The Double Hook*, also explores Watson's sense that language, and thus metaphor and art, define the essence of humanity. However, Watson has not yet made the link between language and discursive universes: *Deep Hollow Creek* does not articulate the new world conditions that ground *The Double Hook*, nor evoke the later novel's apocalyptic tensions. Although Watson is determined in *The Double Hook* to show that the new world's attempt to create itself is not impossible, she is equally determined to make her readers understand that the success of that attempt is not automatic or easy: her expression of its positive possibility does not altogether secure it. The deadly seriousness with which she invests the language of the text remains. Language is uncomfortably unstable, and the meddling with the foundations of the world still frets about the edges of the work.

It is precisely this tension within *The Double Hook* that makes the novel a paradigm of the process of creating the new world in discourse. The conflict demonstrated by Watson's attention to the two registers of the text reveals the centrality of *The Double Hook* in Canadian discursive construction and cultural practice. Watson provokes questions of being, knowing, and meaning on a personal, community, and cultural level, and provides the only possible answers – silence and insensibility – in the absence of a functioning discursive framework. She shows the result of this absence: the cosmos does not signify the validity of human existence; reality is not humanly meaningful; all "truths" are individual, relative, and unsustaining; human beings exist in inarticulate confusion and solipsism. Collapse is imminent at the point where the reader enters the text: matricide provokes the terror of chaos.

The Double Hook questions the fundamental structures of being and achieves the remarkable feat of simultaneously enacting and interrogating that construction: the subject of the work becomes its own process. Richardson's and Grove's literary works exhibit their own particular tensions because of the circumstances of the place in their time; Watson is exercised by analogous factors, but she is also deliberately subversive in her dismantling of the normative texts of Western culture. She will not allow her text to leave this challenge to reality and meaning unanswered: she *chooses* to place the anxiety in her text that Richardson and Grove *must* exert on theirs. Richardson and Grove do not have Watson's sophisticated awareness of the new world predicament; their texts begin under a pressure to find the end and to close rather than open the questions that could destroy both them and their worlds. Watson seems to refuse the psychic nightmares that the new world causes for Richardson and Grove, yet the threat attending their new world is real for hers as well. *The Double Hook* begins by immediately evoking both registers on which the text exists; it ends by allowing narrative closure to reflect the transformation of void into presence and silence into speech resonant with transcendent meaning. It makes us see that the new world exists only as it is spoken, written, invented in language.

In Watson's terms the dilemma is the meaning that language can grant or deny, and is enormously charged with the questions of structure, of content, of what is central for a culture to know. If all social arrangements are discourse, the question of how the discourse of literature reflects this country's social arrangements is answered in *The Double Hook*. Watson shows very clearly the difficult process of retaining or replacing givens, of accommodating the contents of different histories into a relationship with each other while maintaining a delicate balance in a world that threatens to disintegrate under the extreme pressure of that activity. The conflict in the two levels of the text is indicative of the conditions that inform the new world. By existing in the gap between the discursive constructions of old and new worlds, *The Double Hook* both performs and embodies the cultural and linguistic practice of the new world. The setting on soft ground, the threat of the slide into non-meaning, reveal the silence and absence between worlds, the discursive construction of a culture and literature, and the tentative nature of that construction.

CHAPTER FIVE

Robert Kroetsch:
Re-placing Language

While Watson moves between literal and metaphoric planes in her dismantling and construction of new world discourse, Robert Kroetsch's work inhabits both. Watson shows the process of discursive construction in the new world; Kroetsch places the new discursive structure. His work presents the physical reality of the western Canadian landscape, often recognizable, often with actual place names. Yet the act of placing human beings and a cultural structure in that landscape is not literal or realistic. The imaginative and intellectual processes of inhabitation and claiming that Kroetsch's fiction performs are grounded in a place that becomes more real in fiction than in fact. Kroetsch says his fiction-writing is shaped by his Canadian experience (*Creation* 53); his work demonstrates his assumption that writing springs from a sense of place, and the writing that comes *from* a place is the writing *of* that place (Ball 21). The space/place transformation can only occur discursively: Kroetsch's work proves his contention that the fiction makes us – and the new world – real (*Creation* 63).

One of Kroetsch's most famous and familiar critical statements is the title of his 1974 essay "Unhiding the Hidden: Recent Canadian Fiction." In the essay Kroetsch connects Heidegger's comment on the "rootlessness of Western thought," which begins with the translation of Greek words into Roman, with Canadian writing: "The Canadian writer's particular predicament is that he works with a language, within a literature, that appears to be authentically his own, and not a borrowing. But just as there was in the Latin word a concealed Greek experience, so there is in the Canadian word a concealed other experience, sometimes British, sometimes

American" (58). In this statement Kroetsch also connects language with culture, colonialism, and the particular new world condition of Canada. Kroetsch understands the condition of language in the new world and the particular forms in which the playing out of that problematic can occur. The new world is controlled and lost in its naming: the name replaces what it is meant to represent. The dialectic of place and displacement begins here; this lack of linguistic fit (Ashcroft, Griffiths, Tiffin 25) is in Kroetsch's view the source of Canadian writers' preoccupation with landscape, and the subject of his own writing. To inhabit the new world, Canadian writers must "uninvent the world" – unname, demythologize, erase the prior inscriptions before beginning again to name, invent, speak. Kroetsch recognizes that to uninvent the word is to uninvent the world (Introduction to *Boundary* 2 1); he shares something of Watson's sense of the consequences of unravelling the world and of the play that the silent point allows, and like her he refuses certainty of meaning for either writer or reader. Kroetsch's way out of what he calls the paradox of Canadian writing is to enter it: in refusing the borrowed words and in grounding his writing in this culture and this place, Kroetsch moves *through* the silence that threatens to annihilate Watson's figures. The new world is invented in its renaming, made real as it becomes both itself and something else: the new world is *both* a place and a discursive construct.

Kroetsch's sense of the integral relationship between writing and its ground or place results in his figure of archaeology, one basis of his discursive conception of the new world. The archaeological metaphor signals the many senses of his investigation of place and recalls the primary act of inscription in *The Double Hook*: the old lady dragging her hook across the mud bed of the lake. Kroetsch does not uncover or reveal any primary acts in this sense – in his new world there are none – but instead finds layers of inscriptions and significations that work against any notion of a singular, authoritative reality and call up the possibility of the many rewritings that exist in the ambivalent neither/nor conditions of the new world. The world is spoken and written into existence, but in a multiplicity of voices and realities: archaeology accepts the violence of the discontinuity of form ("Porcupine" 111–12) and allows for the fragmented nature of the story rather than demanding or reinforcing the coerced unity of traditional history ("Alberta Writer" 76). It also allows Kroetsch to make the place in language and to work within and against the conventions of the landscape and of writing about it, as well as to link that placement to literary theory. Kroetsch's postmodernism and his concern with the cultural and physical entity converge in the archaeological metaphor and in the Canadian west.

Robert Lecker argues that the nature of Kroetsch's creative work has inspired particular types of criticism and that Kroetsch himself is responsible for "instill[ing] a new critical vocabulary in a receptive audience" (*Kroetsch* 123). Ann Mandel observes that Kroetsch's essays "creatively turn Canadian writers and texts into voices preparing a way in the wilderness for his own coming. He arrives by coming first" (55). John Clement Ball comments that Kroetsch is "his own best explicator" and makes the further point that there is a certain cohesiveness to Kroetsch's work, as his ideas echo back and forth between his work as writer and as critic (1). Certainly this reflexivity is apparent in *Gone Indian*, the third novel of Kroetsch's out-west triptych, in which he uses techniques of deconstruction and metafiction to make a novel out of critical commentary on a taped text: an American graduate student travels to the Canadian northwest, tape-records for his supervisor the insights that might help him to write his dissertation, and eventually disappears in a carnivalistic Babel that is, again, familiar to readers of Kroetsch's critical commentary and fiction. Personal identity and cultural stereotypes are undone here, as are the literary and academic figurings of the male quest, the American dream, the frontier thesis, and the novel form itself. Kroetsch's fiction in this context is, of course, more than metafictional: *Gone Indian* interrogates not only the processes of both academic and creative writing but also the radical transformation of being and identity allowed and required by the new world as well. The novel is explicitly an exercise in discursive invention of personal identity and the new world: one of the protagonist's unfinished dissertations begins with "Christopher Columbus, not knowing that he had not come to the Indies, named the inhabitants of that new world –" (21). Like Columbus, on his trip into unknown territory Jeremy does not know where he has landed. He remains nowhere until he realizes that this world cannot be discovered but must be invented. In his invention of the Canadian northwest, Jeremy invents himself as well, and leaves the text.

The first invention of Jeremy occurs in his naming – by his father, for Jeremy Bentham – in the hope that the child will become a professor. This naming directs Jeremy into years of unsuccessful academic work, until he realizes that he cannot or need not be determined by "the accident of his name: that one portion of identity which is at once so totally invented and so totally real" (51). As he abandons that naming – by forgetting it, by answering the Edmonton customs officer's "Purpose of trip?" with "I want to be Grey Owl ... I want to become –" (6) – he begins the process of stripping off layers of inauthentic naming. The new name he wants is, again, someone else's, and already a fictional and cultural renaming. It has also been Jeremy's imposed and then chosen disguise since his childhood: "I didn't want to be the Indian at all. They told me, You be the Indian, Sadness. We'll hunt you down. No matter where you hide, we'll hunt you down. We'll kill you. And they threw broken bricks and they tied me up ... So the tailor across the hall from my mother's apartment brought me in his books of Grey Owl; one by one, he brought them. Unfolded them. Unveiled them. He gave me his dream of the European boy who became ... pathfinder ... borderman ... the truest Indian of them all. When I was old enough, brave enough, a teaching assistantship in my bedroll, I fled Greenwich Village ... Yes, to the wilderness" (94). In refusing one borrowed name and accepting another, Jeremy acquires a model and metaphor of behaviour; in the new world setting his childhood literary hero, the Englishman who became Grey Owl, is uncannily appropriate. Archie Belaney invented his own new world name and identity, and ironically became famous for his books about life in the wilderness. In his "I want to be Grey Owl ... I want to become –" Jeremy is not simply saying that he wants to be something or someone else: his choice of model shows that he is already constructing an imaginative version of the self in a complex autobiographical act *and* within a literary frame. We are immediately informed, then, that Jeremy's act is fictive and discursive.

The site of his act is implicated in this discursive construction as well. Jeremy can play the Indian "for real" only in the new world setting that allows precisely that transformation of identity and reality, a world that can be spoken into existence and in which a self can be created out of a suitcase. Jeremy's Grey Owl metamorphosis occurs on the last frontier of the new world: the northwest combines both Canadian and American understandings of frontier and is a place where transformation, if not commonplace, is at least not unprecedented.

"Sadness," old Madham says to me one day, "there's only one problem in this world that you take seriously."

"Right," I said.

"No," he said. "I mean yes. Why did Archie Belaney become Grey Owl?"

"How," I said. I raised my right hand, the palm facing the good professor's beaming face. Why he was sweating I do not know.

"The story of a man," I agreed, "who died into a new life."

"He faked the death."

"But he woke up free nevertheless."

"Be serious."

"One false move, Professor, and instead of addressing you, I'll be you. That's serious."   (62)

Jeremy and Madham are already very close to exchanging or at least sharing identities: Madham is obsessed with Jeremy's trip and tapes because it is his own transformation in reverse that Jeremy is enacting and recording. Madham casts Jeremy's trip to "his" northwest as a fulfilment of Jeremy's childhood dream, but clearly it is his own quest that Jeremy fulfils vicariously for him: "I sent him out there as on a mission, as on a veritable quest for something forever lost to me and yet recoverable to the world" (13–14). That something lost to Madham is not only his western life, including his wife, with whom Jeremy disappears at the end of the novel, but his ego as well: Kroetsch makes the Madham/Jeremy transformation the first step in Jeremy's journey into multiple possibilities.

That first step is complicated by Madham's own transformation. Madham's past and his complicity in Jeremy's trip are revealed by his numerous clues to his own first name and identity: Robert Sunderman, the young man who disappeared while playing hockey on a frozen slough. He and Sunderman both have "the perfect physique"; Madham is the same age as Sunderman would be; at the end of the novel Madham grieves that Worlds End, which he has come to love as well as if it were his own (154), is deserted.[1] When he says that Jeremy dreamed northwest, he says of himself, "I am a western boy who ever dreamed east" (95): "The forest of my own intent is inhabited by strange creatures, surely. The figure of Roger Dorck for one comes to haunt me. He was a dedicated man who spent his life caring for the family of a drowned friend. I cannot for a moment accept the notion that his 'accident' was motivated by disappointment in love. Accident is a part of our daily lives; if not, then all of modern physics is madness. Are not explanations themselves assigned almost at random?" (51) Of course Madham assigns explanations at random to Jeremy's actions, but Kroetsch is pointing up a more widespread disorder, which only begins in the sharing of intent and identity between Madham and Jeremy: it develops with the expansion of the Jeremy/Madham/Sunderman triad.

Jeremy eventually stops trying to become Madham and to enact the academic role, and becomes the discarded identity, Sunderman, instead. But this is immediately complicated and enlarged by the events at the Edmonton airport, in which identity is not simply shared but diffused: Jeremy forgets his name, is detained with a transvestite smuggler who claims to have been a buffalo in a previous life, is mistaken for Roger Dorck, whose luggage he has acquired by accident, and leaves the airport disguised as himself. The series of events thus started cannot be stopped. The ending occurs early in the novel, on page 23 – "Mr. Dorck must have read in this notebook, trying to discover who took his suitcase. And he printed across the bottom of the page: 'THIS, THEN, IS HOW IT ENDED'"– and the story continues in multiplying layers of doubling and repetition: the cowboy and Roger Dorck are both injured by wild Icarus flights and falls; Dorck is Bea's lover both before she marries Sunderman and after his disappearance, and Jeremy replaces Dorck with Bea and as Winter King; Sunderman telephoned Bea after his disappearance, which is re-enacted when Jeremy calls for Dorck after Dorck's accident; Bea's daughter becomes Dorck's lover after Bea's disappearance because he thinks she is a younger Bea; Bea disappears as her husband did, while Carol says that *she* would have gone with her husband; Madham replaces Jeremy with his wife, while Jeremy replaces Madham/Sunderman with his; Madham, with Carol, acts out the buffalo mating that Jeremy dreams; Carol is the same age as Madham/Sunderman's daughter Jill. Jeremy is acting out Madham's conflicting desire to return to the unlimited possibilities of a disordered realm, which he will not undertake precisely because of "the consequence of the northern prairies to human definition: the diffusion of personality into a complex of possibilities rather than a concluded self" (152). Madham will not risk that diffusion – even though he may occasionally be "suffocating ... saturated, walled in, drowning" (152), he will not go back. In contrast, Jeremy

desires precisely that freedom from the limits of names and associated behaviours. Kroetsch provides it for him in the metaphor of
the carnival.

Kroetsch's interpretation of the carnival is informed by his reading
of Mikhail Bakhtin: the carnival allows the changes in identity,
perception, and shared reality that Kroetsch wants us to understand
are also allowed – or required – by the new world. While performing
Roger Dorck's role of the Winter King in the Notikeewin Winter
Festival, Jeremy finds the carnival world. He also re-enacts Dorck's
snowmobile accident and finds another parallel reality under the
snow, which interprets for him the conditions under which his ego
can now exist: "Snow on my eyelashes told me that I was inside a
snowman, looking out on a strange, distant world ... You are right
to make the last entry and close the notebook, let the pencil slip
from your hand. You have only to listen now. Say no more. Listen
to the fall of silence, hear your own last breath and know for one
instant you are no longer" (40). He then runs the snowshoe race,
although he has never worn snowshoes before, "like a bear that was
learning to dance" (82). Loping like a coyote, swerving with a rabbit,
following a magpie, he outdistances the other runners and names
the landscape he is running through: "I dodged around a crater in
the snow; a dip, I decided, that must conceal a buffalo wallow. A
lone tree in the distance was a rubbing tree. I decided that too"
(85). He is linked to that landscape – swearing he "could smell the
blood of a buffalo jump" (85), he stumbles, and realizes that he
does not want to win or even finish the race: "I took great solace
from the recollection of [Zeno's] arrow. I looked at my feet, forever
dividing the space between me and my goal. I will never get there,
don't worry, I told myself" (87). The snowshoe race foreshadows
Jeremy's subsequent transformations and eventual disappearance:

I had left the mere earth, you understand. I was travelling above the snow,
light-footed on strange slippers ... I was no longer merely thinking. My
mind was the landscape ... My body was totally spent. And thus I was
free of my body. There was no goal now: I was following the magpie. And
yet he was in my head ... The snow below us was a great bed. Only by
some impossible effort could we reach it. Our straining lifted us up and
outward. Away. We struggled to get down to the beautiful white sheets,
the pillows of white. Which were also in my head. I could not stop the
struggle downward, which took me up. Which was all in my head.   (88)

By the end of the novel there is no separation between the world and what is in Jeremy's head. As the magpie flies off into space at the end of the race, Jeremy is pulled down, fighting to free himself. Surrounded by the men who look like muskrats and who want an explanation of his identity and the strategy of his win, he intuits what will be his last recorded act in his text: "I wanted to start up and fly. This whole damned country, I thought to myself, they're all trying to vanish into the air. Like that magpie. Like that cowboy, a sunfishing bronco wasn't enough, he had to take flight from a catapult. And Dorck himself. Leaping, leaping, launching out over the cliff's edge, his red suit zippered against the wind, he would rise up and up and up and up –" (91). At this point Jeremy does not fly but is sufficiently distanced from earthly reality to be unable to speak: "Again I did not answer. When I might have saved myself, simply by speaking. But I would not speak. For if I had tried, it would have been a tongue I did not understand" (93). His not-speaking appears to confirm his Indian identity, and he is beaten for winning the race. Jeremy's next transformations complete the cycle of unnaming and renaming: he becomes first a buffalo bull, then Has-Two-Chances, and finally turns off the tape recorder.

Jeremy's metamorphosis into a fake North American native is in part Kroetsch's satiric play on white ethnocentrism and romanticism, just as Jeremy's pilgrimage from upstate New York to the Canadian northwest is an ironic inversion of the American dream. But Kroetsch also suggests that some basic aspect of the new world personality is expressed in this fictive, scripted invention. The issue of identity and its mediation in discourse define Jeremy well before he encounters either the carnival or the northwest. His idea of what he, now called Grey Owl, should look like is both a disguise and an autobiographical text that Madham reads as the savage: "He is sloppy, uptight, unclean: your version of a savage ... Jeremy is unshaven and wears no shirt over his bare chest. He has come in out of the icy sunlight in his levis and moccasins and his buckskin jacket. For your scalp. For your maidenhood" (21–2). In his Grey Owl outfit the imposter's imposter is taken for the real thing: Jeremy's naïveté allows him to enact the role of the winning Indian that Joe Beaver avoids by throwing the dogsled race.

But Kroetsch also suggests that it is precisely the discursive element of Jeremy's and Grey Owl's act that allows them to overcome the displacement the other European inhabitants of the new world suffer: that a self constructed in this way most fully inhabits the new world of European invention. There is another sense, too, in which Kroetsch's contemplation of the construction of self and place repeats Richardson's questioning of savagery and civilization and the associated notions of human nature and behaviour allowed and provoked by the new world. In Richardson's view, Wacousta's "going Indian" is clearly beyond, although fundamentally related to, the limits of civilized human behaviour; it is also clear that the new world setting allows that movement beyond limits to occur. Richardson and Kroetsch are both fascinated by this border. Jeremy calls the Indian the borderman: the new world native is transformed into the literary figure of metaphor to describe a discursive act. In this sense, then, Jeremy and Grey Owl *are* the truest "Indians" of them all. The metaphor of self, constructed in a literary trope, is the basis of Richardson's, Kroetsch's, and Grey Owl's texts – and Grove's, whose discursive act comes to mind in this context. Like the reborn Grove, Jeremy is the quintessential Kroetsch hero, acting out not the quest for identity as the given authentic self but the belief that the chosen fiction is the fullest and most free imaginative act (Thomas *Kroetsch* 3). What Kroetsch says of Grove applies equally to Jeremy: "As his reality, so to speak, comes into doubt, he comes more and more to represent our own predicament" ("Canadian Writer" 56). The natives in the novel see through Jeremy's disguise – Joe Beaver's children ask why Jeremy's hair is that way (65) – when it is simply a disguise. But the validation of his true transformation comes from the same source, when, after the beating, Joe Beaver and his wife dress him in a *real* Indian's (Joe's) clothes and tell him that he has become the real imposter: "Grey Owl would be proud ... He was brave like you" (100–1).

There is, then, more to Kroetsch's treatment of the European impulse to "go Indian" than irony. Kroetsch is serious in showing that the movement beyond known limits is also a movement into what Europeans in the new world cannot know except in discursive terms. After the beating and the dressing in Joe's clothes, Jeremy unnames himself again into a buffalo bull and dreams the undoing of the European settlement of North America: "And the buffalo came back in his dreaming. Out of the north they came ... And the herds moved onto the bald prairies. The wheatfields were gone ... Tell the Bloods. The cattle are gone from the prairie ranches; the ranches are gone. Tell the Piegans. The wolves are come from the north, are waiting to eat. The grizzly comes down from the western mountains. Tell the Stonies to build the buffalo pound. Tell the squaws to gather buffalo chips. Tell the dogs to be silent. Tell the hunter to get for his medicine bundle FIRST a decorated pipestem, THEN ... the skin of a grey owl" (101–3). Jeremy's entry into a new world identity that has no words allows him access to history as well as to a new future. Early in the novel he states his desire to find the beginning: "I am looking for nothing. The primal darkness. The purest light. For the first word. For the voice that spoke the first word. The inventor of zero" (22). The assumptions and conclusions demanded by the old world framing of new world experience within historical discourse are precisely what Jeremy and Kroetsch refuse: Kroetsch's archaeological and unhiding metaphors converge here to create the possibility of a new history.

The enabling context of the buffalo dream leads Jeremy forward to his penultimate transformation and renaming: "'Now,' [Poundmaker] said, 'you are Has-Two-Chances.' It was as if the calling of the name itself awakened him ... he found himself in a dark so dark he might have been in a womb. Dreaming the world to come" (106). Dreaming backwards in the "virulence and vise of his fatal impulse to seek out the unknown" (72), Jeremy, with Columbus, invents his own new world: "The Columbus quest for the oldest New World. The darkest gold. The last first. I was lifting my hidden face. To the gateway beyond. To the place of difficult entrance. To the real gate to the dreamed cave ... I had tongued the unspeakable silence" (147). Jeremy's simultaneous inventions of new world and self, expressed in the sexual metaphor, is a radical joining of language, history, and reality:

And that was when I recognized: I will never ever get out of bed, get up again. Never. Not ever. I am bed-bound. Freed finally from the curse of locomotion. Ha. The free man freed from his freedom. The curse cursed. Yes. Now. I shall, at last, commence my dissertation. Christopher Columbus, not knowing that he had not come to the Indies of his imagination. Imagined that he had come to the Indies.

Right on, Sadness. Dead center. The beautiful truth ... I am landing all over again ... The mechanical voice has got to be kidding: Edmonton International Airport it says, in English, then in French. Down below our jet engines we see nothing but snow-drifted fields. The setting sun a blood clot in my own glass skull. The small earth downward and darkly white –

Blank.

I lie here. Ha. I am going to lie here for the rest of my life, talking, recording everything. Until I can think nothing that I do not speak. Speaking. Until the inside and the outside are one, united – (149)

When the inside and the outside are one, Jeremy turns off the tape recorder and moves out of the text that his recorded speaking has made possible; Kroetsch prefigured this act earlier when Jeremy reached through the mirror to touch his own skin, feared that Dorck's suitcase contained his own possessions, and began his series of metamorphoses.

Jeremy's Columbus act draws us back to O'Gorman's argument about the invention of the Americas in language: the continental landmass in the Atlantic only became "America" when it was so named, or, to use Nietzsche's phrase, the name is what first makes a thing visible (quoted in Ruland 6). Although the world is enlarged by such an act, there is also some loss of firm ground in that naming. Jeremy dreaming backward to the Columbus moment demonstrates Kroetsch's later comment that "in Canada, uncertain of the canon, we write commentaries on the process of creation itself" ("Journals" 148), which reminds us of what Bhabha calls the familiar quest for origin in new cultures. All the novels in this study are such commentaries, from Richardson's new world nightmare to Urquhart's interrogation of the status of all forms of speaking and knowing in the new world.

In his taped commentary Jeremy is freed into a final unnaming and undoing of history:

Freed finally ... into bed ... forever ... until a new ice age ... the slow southward push ... I refuse ... the glacier itself, nudging the bedpost ... slowly ... I refuse ... forcing the bed itself, sideways, up ... CAN YOU HEAR ME? ... the old glacier itself, the primal stuff in primal motion ... come back ... slowly breaking my happy trance ... the tumble and rattle of terminal moraine, the distant thunder of ice; cracking ... the immeasurable assault ... COME BACK ... the tongue of ice slipping over the horizon's lip ... slanting away from the Pole itself ... the blue-green flame advancing ... the river of ice ... the rammed, blunt needle – (150; Kroetsch's ellipses)

Jeremy escapes from the text into prehistory and *story*: "The rest is fiction" (157). In an essay titled "No Name Is My Name"

Kroetsch says that "at its best, the threat of anonymity generates story" (51). Jeremy's story *is* a story, a fictive construct, and may have provoked Kroetsch's insight that "narrative is more significant than meaning" ("Journals" 140). Kroetsch cites Northrop Frye's famous statement that the Canadian sensibility "is less perplexed by the question 'Who am I?' than by some such riddle as 'Where is here?'" ("No Name" 41); Kroetsch's own unriddling of "whatever it is to be a Canadian" (41) and of the new world leads Jeremy to avoid any name at all. Kroetsch says that such an avoidance does not "deprive one of any identity; indeed, it may offer a plurality of identities" (52). Certainly it does offer that plurality to Jeremy, whose final transformation is into fiction, the title of the novel. Jeremy's world is discursive: this text supremely contains the idea not of world but of book ("Fear of Women" 74). To go Indian is Jeremy's fictive naming: the fiction makes him real and opens, rather than closes, the possibility of more stories and future rewritings.

Kroetsch says that "the novel uniquely confronts the human experience of time and space" ("Journals" 140). The space in which Jeremy's and the new world's discursive conditions exist is, as is obvious by now, particular and unique. In this peculiar land where illusion is "rife" (8), physical reality must be created discursively: "That's when the driver said, 'Notikeewin.' As if by speaking the name he had created a place on the blank earth" (16). Kroetsch suggests that the world thus created can disappear again, as can Jeremy: "[The telegraph poles] made me notice the space – they or their shadows on the snow, on the horizon – and I couldn't even pretend to sleep. Because if I did I might wink out and be gone forever" (15). That is exactly what Jeremy eventually does. As Sunderman goes east and becomes Madham, Jeremy goes further north: perhaps through the ice into the Cree River and on to Hudson Bay and the "drifting arctic wastes" (157), perhaps not; perhaps accidentally, perhaps not. Kroetsch suggests that their departures are similar – Sunderman leaves a hole in the ice while Jeremy's tape recorder is left hanging from a bridge over a frozen river – and predicts their ends early in the book: "[Jill] knocked a hole in the ice with [her] laugh. [Jeremy] leaped. He plunged in at the broken edge. Returned, returned. Into the bath of cold, and down. The white world around him turning black" (43). Kroetsch has Jeremy say: "It was my own theory at the time that man living in wide-open spaces had a different relation to objects: because he could see where he stood, where he was going" (87). Jeremy certainly has a different clarity of vision in the northwest, which allows his transformations. Madham explains the mysteries of the place in terms of physical conditions and ascribes to Jeremy the symptoms of Arctic hysteria: "The extreme cold, the long nights, the solitude of *unbounded* space: these are the enemies that induce that northern ecstasy ... At any rate, the afflicted person, quite commonly, senses the presence of another who is not in fact there" (123–4). The other is, in fact, the landscape itself: "You were covered in snow, Jeremy and you. You were moving landscapes" (57). Where person and place are interchangeable, time is disrupted as well. At World's/Worlds End all the clocks are stopped until Jeremy restarts them, with this result: "The clocks are striking. One of them says it is six o'clock. One of them says it is either midnight or noon" (149). Madham leaves to escape being "*trapped* in the blank indifference of space and timelessness" (124), which can either invent the new world or annihilate the concluded self.

The form of the novel addresses the idea of the concluded self. Kroetsch's play with autobiography, fiction, and the roles of speaker and subject is a commentary in itself on the process of literary creation and discursive construction: as Jeremy and Madham speak and write, they invent themselves, a text, and the discourse in which both they and the new world can exist. The narrative is constructed by Madham as he transcribes Jeremy's tapes and edits the resulting text: "Of course I have had to select from the tapes, in spite of Jeremy's instructions to the contrary: the mere onslaught of detail merely overwhelms" (13). Madham's is the controlling consciousness of the novel; through his slanted telling of the narrative the reader comes to question not only Madham's assumptions and beliefs but the reader's own perceptions, as well as the place and experience that suddenly become new. Kroetsch's deconstruction of narratorial reliability and autobiographical form here recalls the earlier novels of the triptych, particularly Demeter Proudfoot in his empty bathtub supposedly telling the story of Hazard Lepage in *The Studhorse Man*. By insisting that Jeremy perished in the fall from the railway bridge rather than escaped under the snow and ice, Madham tries to deny Jeremy's possible metamorphosis into Madham himself and to distinguish between Jeremy as speaking subject and Jeremy as object of Madham's own narrative construction. Instead, as he creates Jeremy he reveals himself: "Is it not odd, this impulse in the erring man: this need to divulge, to confess? This little need assumed immense proportions as Jeremy let himself be propelled by unconscious desires into self-revelation. To get into a corner on those vast prairies is not easy. And yet the words of self-betrayal flowed like a spring flood, like the waters from a breached dam, rolling and tossing and breaking a lost body into oblivion" (95–6).

What Madham says about Jeremy can be said of himself: the entire novel is a function of his own need to confess. Jeremy and Madham are each both character and storyteller in this record of their own and each other's lives; Madham as critic and editor adds the academic functions that Jeremy is unable to master. Jeremy's ability to complete the academic exercise is made personal and autobiographical by the role-models – Jeremy Bentham and Madham himself – he tries to emulate, while his ability to invent his fictive self is so mediated by his academic training that Madham's advice to use the tape recorder may be better than Madham intends. But the goal of both the academic and autobiographical discourses in this context is not to find voice but to lose it: Kroetsch's deliberate undercutting of authorial control and presence is expressed in the doubled and then multiplied names and voices that produce the text and the silent absence with which it ends.

Gone Indian raises the question of the nature of the new world's existence. If self and place are discursive inventions, clearly both can be spoken out of as well as into being: Jeremy stops talking when the inside and the outside become one and leaves the text, while Madham, like Grove, writes incessantly. The new world's promise of possibility exists precisely in the possibilities of discursive invention. The fact that Kroetsch's northwest exists only in his, Madham's, and Jeremy's words explains the instability of Richardson's world and confirms Grove's and Watson's intuitions about autobiographical and literary discourses in the new world; it remains for Urquhart to see what these new world conditions do to other special discourses, narratives, and voices. Kroetsch's work shares the dialectic of place and displacement of these other writers and speaks across the gap to place the discursive structure of the new world. If writing reinvents the world, reading reinvents the text. Kroetsch's poetry, fiction, and criticism function as commentary and extension of each other because all are part of the discourse, what he calls the story: "It's the story, its treatment, the narrative itself, that's the model, not an outside conception ... I think criticism is really a version of story, you see; I think we are telling the story to each other of how we get at story" (*Labyrinths* 30).

He is also telling the story of how we get at the new world. E.D. Blodgett argues that the frontiers of the English-speaking west were drawn in linear patterns of railway, survey lines, and sections that enforced a geographic and psychological closure even as they opened the region, and extends this contradiction to include a further one between the geometric design of place and the genres of English Canadian fiction of the west. In one sense the linear design applies to *Gone Indian*: Jeremy states his horror of "the inevitable circle" (144) just before he vanishes, and his movement throughout the novel is not cyclic. The point, however, is made explicit that linearity does not require closure. It is precisely this contradiction between the perception of place and the manner in which place is presented in literature that Kroetsch addresses here. Jeremy wants to go further, and in the new world's discursive conditions, he can. Kroetsch believes the absence of limit is the presence of possibility: in Madham's words, getting into a corner on the prairie is difficult (95). For Kroetsch, and for Jeremy, then, "to go west [is] to enter the mind's geometry, a long journey, one might say, of self-reflection, of finding one's self lost" (Blodgett "Geometry" 215). We might substitute new world for west. Because Kroetsch makes the place more real in language than in fact, Jeremy can transfigure himself out of it. Embracing fictionality, the fiction becomes *fiction* and at the same time becomes more *real* than fiction.

Kroetsch insists on the connection between language and physical and cultural place, which places us immediately on the discursive plane: this is culture-making at the level of language. As a textual and cultural construction *Gone Indian* moves into a more complete possession of its place than any of the earlier texts discussed here, while continuing to show the tentativeness of any such act. A problem of language is a problem of culture, identity, and literature – Kroetsch's "How do you write in a new country?" is a serious question. One answer is that there is nothing to write about (*Labyrinths* 145): "Canadian literature, at its most radical, is the autobiography of a culture that tells its story by telling us repeatedly it has no story to tell" ("Veil" 193). The other answer – Jeremy's and Madham's – is that the new world's discursive invention *is* the story itself.

CHAPTER SIX

Jane Urquhart:
Writing the New World

Jane Urquhart's novel *The Whirlpool* is a paradigm of the enterprise of the new world writer and a self-conscious contemplation of the effects of new world conditions on the formation and functioning of special discourses. Like Kroetsch, Urquhart uses the act of writing as the structural and theoretical basis of her text. She centres the novel on forms of writing and shows the impossibility of conceiving of the new world in traditional intellectual categories: the new world's discursive ordering is radically new. The novel's characters are all engaged in recording new world experience and discover that their borrowed discursive forms are dysfunctional in this place: the historian cannot read the signs of history that surround him; the poet cannot find Wordsworth's daffodils in the Gatineau Hills or in the bush around Niagara; the archivist cannot discover or impose order on a collection of artifacts; the diarist exits the text. The resulting absence of control, order, and structure energizes Urquhart's text as it does Watson's and Kroetsch's.

Like Kroetsch's, Urquhart's title is a metaphor of the text's new world condition: as the movement of the whirlpool mixes its waters and fragments the bodies of the floaters, the new world dissolves the traditional boundaries between discourses and blends history with fiction, reality with imagination. The temptation to order and classify within systems of knowledge is refused by the whirlpool's contradictory movement; finality and authority contradict and threaten the condition and experience of the new world and under-line the imaginative and metaphorical conditions of its inhabitation. As Urquhart grounds the text in discursive acts, she exhibits the new world writer's preoccupation with systems of ordering and understanding; the sudden instability of such systems reveals the radical consequences of the new world's discursive nature. Her own writing performs the imaginative act of invention and inhabitation: in revealing its discursive nature, she writes the new world.

Urquhart uses the novel's characters to work out her ideas about discourse in the new world. She is especially interested in history and literature: her new world "historical" novel, set in 1889, is framed by old world poets. The two professional and published writers in the new world, the historian and the poet, think that their special discourses both provide and express a controlling structure that they find personally and culturally sustaining. David's historical work will, he insists, complete the War of 1812. He is determined that, despite the 342 American books on the subject, the truth will be known: the Canadians won the war and the Americans retreated. His work is motivated by a dream in which Laura Secord, his heroine of the war, tells him *"Remind them, remind them"* (83). He does not simply research and write about the war but lives it – "he could actually feel the regimental energy flow from his pen, almost as if he, himself, were inventing the plan of attack" (49); he spends his days immersed in his historical work and his evenings giving lectures in which he exhorts his audience to "think Canadian" and fantasizing his wife Fleda into Laura Secord, ostensibly to inspire his work.

His desire to make Fleda into Secord reveals a basic contradiction: he wants to live out the dramas of the past he researches because, unlike his own life, the ending is already known. He also wants to impose that closure on a public and national level in his production of the true account of Canada's past. David actually wants "to make a museum ... a better museum" (210), but he cannot read the historical artifacts that do not conform to his notions of order or yield easily to his interpretation: the bullet-hole in General Brock's uniform; Brock's hat, several sizes too large, which arrived too late for his last battle; the cannon-balls Maud digs up in her garden, the site of the Battle of Lundy's Lane, which he collects for what purposes neither of them knows. The record of the war, kept by the quilt of a woman who lived through it, defeats him entirely:

David moved even closer to the object until he could see evidence of missing stitches in the spot where the coffins had been removed, had been taken into the velvet graveyard.

"My God," he whispered, "Why on earth ...?"

"Why not?" Fleda turned to look directly at him. "Why not? How could all this sewing be any worse than the reality of –"

"But it's so calculated, as if this woman knew that everybody was going to die."

"Everybody is going to die."

"But it's almost as if she caused it."

"No, David, the war caused it; she recorded it." (173)

What David misses here is the causal agency, as well as the pain. He mistakes the function of the woman's quilt, which only records the reality of the deaths that men have caused, a reality that escapes him in his historical research, along with the blood (127). War for him is "*an abstract theory meaning something else entirely*" (198), important only as material for his work (209).

David welcomes what he perceives to be the peace, stasis, and containment of the museum and its artifacts, and mistakenly seeks his wife there after she disappears. He finds instead only inarticulate and unintelligible artifacts. He insists on a closed narrative: he will not honour fragmentariness and confusion, nor admit the subjectivity of his records. More importantly, though, neither will he allow that the construction of history, like the construction of the new world itself, is a human activity that gains its meaning from its awareness of itself as a human construct. David's failure of imagination and inability to understand a metaphoric record of history are emblematic of what happens in his marriage. His attempt to write his wife into his romanticized and eroticized version of Laura Secord fails, as does his attempt to fit her into someone else's text, Patmore's *Angel in the House*. Fleda refuses both scriptings and, like Jeremy in *Gone Indian*, walks out of the text. When she disappears, David's fixed ideas about national treacheries lead him to suspect that something "American" has happened to her. His facts come to be insubstantial, like Patrick's: "History, his story, whose story? Collections of facts that were really only documented rumours. When he thought hard about them, thought hard about facts, they evaporated under his scrutiny" (72). David disallows knowing through imagination or creativity and discounts the effect of imagination on historical record. For him new world legend is indecipherable unless translated into facts that make the events of this nation's past as solid as those of the old world's.

Through David's character and profession Urquhart is exploring the relationship between history and imagination in the particular circumstances of the new world: specifically, she is questioning the way we create the new world and the record of its past, as well as the manner in which our cultural constructions present that process. The results of her inquiry are crucial to an understanding of the intellectual reordering demanded by the new world; the questions Urquhart forces are both posed and answered by the new world's discursive nature. The novel refuses David's rigid split between ways of knowing and demands the recognition that the knowledge provided by history and the creative imagination is as mixed as the waters in the whirlpool: only in the larger pattern, allowing the validity of both modes, is there any chance at understanding.

Urquhart is positing her own combination of fact and fiction as Canadian legend. Her two source-texts – her husband's grandmother's book of floaters and Julia Cruikshank's 1915 novel *Whirlpool Heights: The Dream-House on the Niagara River* – combine with her own text to show a way of dealing with the past that enlarges rather than restricts, as David's vision does.[1] David's nationalism betrays an insecurity about his new world heritage and is confining, as he allows it to determine his writing of history. He knows the results of his research already: he disregards alternatives and imposes closure on the historical text that he intends will correct the inaccurate American and British records. The problem is that he will never be able to complete the enterprise because it is fundamentally undermined by new world conditions: he cannot interpret the only artifacts that the new world provides as historical "material." Maud has the same problem – her floaters' clothes are as much artifacts as the clothing in David's museum, and just as unreadable. David's obsessive compiling of information reveals both his insecurity and his inability to overcome it: he needs his record to be firmly based on the absolutes that the new world setting makes unavailable. His anxiety results in his phobia of Americans, his attachment to Laura Secord and their shared mission, and his insistence on other-ing his wife into the historical woman. David cannot trust an imaginary woman's ordering of his professional and emotional life through his subconscious and his imagination: he needs her to be tangible and actually present. Neither can he make the shift from the literal to the metaphoric that the new world demands: he cannot understand why his wife's wearing of a muddied calico dress does not bring him closer to his heroine. His way of knowing both Laura Secord and the war is irrelevant and ineffective in the new world – he is a historian who will never *know*, and he does not know why.

The why has to do with the place, which disallows conventional containments of intellectual inquiry – biography, history, "fact." In the new world these categories are meaningless: they no longer hold or offer knowledge or understanding. David is convinced that there is a particular new world personality that expresses itself in "thinking Canadian" and will in time be made manifest in a nation of patriots. He also thinks that there is an essential nature of Canada – and that he *knows* it – which is both expressed and fulfilled in its victory over the United States in the War of 1812; his record of the war, then, will both define and fulfil the nation and secure its past and future. His thinking, however, is tautological and his singularity restricting. His war is not yet over, nor ever will be: his enemy is any questioning of his mode of inquiry or its only possible conclusion, based on verifiable "facts" and polished cannon-balls. His imagination cannot call up a battlefield or conceive of place in terms other than those of his defining methodology: he cannot even get Fleda's dream-house built in the forest above the whirlpool. Unable to think in new world terms, David can "think Canadian" only literally, and accordingly cannot get beyond his obsession with Canada's proximity to the United States or the sense that he and his great work are underrated and misunderstood. As a result, he will never finish the research or begin to write: compiling the papers will "take [him] the rest of [his] life" (84).

Patrick, the other new world writer, is similarly inarticulate. He is silenced by the disjuncture between the ordered European landscape and the Canadian wilderness, figured here as the chaos of the falls and whirlpool in the Niagara River. Canadian landscape defeats him: as his wife predicted, he does not find Wordsworth's daffodils in the Gatineau Hills or in the bush around Niagara. His poetry consists mainly of pine trees: in his attempt to invent place figuratively, he ignores people, an act analogous to David's evocations of battlefields empty of mutilated bodies (125). Patrick tries to organize the natural setting as a landscape and is amazed to find elements in it that he has not placed there: "Until that moment a week earlier, it had never occurred to him that a figure would enter any of his landscapes. They were fierce places, wild with growth, crazy with weather" (55–6). He too tries to construct Fleda as other and equates her with landscape, using his limited language to deny her humanity and voice and transform her into the silent muse of his new world poetry. He gathers up her discarded cut hair and then, in a "metaphoric reference to his own behaviour" (151), takes her and her husband on *"an endless and unsuccessful search for a tiny wild orchid called Ladies' Tresses, which he says blooms only around the U.S./Canadian border"* (150). He is frightened by proximity to both the landscape and Fleda: just as the bend in the current of the whirlpool is practically invisible at close range (79), individual distinction disappears when he is close to Fleda, and threatens him with Kroetsch's diffusion of personality: "when we're this close we can't see each other at all ... not even each other's eyes. This close, you're a blur ... and I'm nothing ... completely nothing ... nothing but a voice. You can't see me. My voice is so close it could be inside your own head" (181; Urquhart's ellipses). Rejecting the woman's separate reality while insisting on his own, he comes to see her as an element of his own making, merged with the whirlpool: "Alone, with his imagination set free, he disregarded all he had seen and heard, and allowed the woman and the whirlpool to combine. By the time he reached his room he had completely reinvented her. He could hardly wait to return to the woods where, hiding once again, he could watch her in the pure and uncorrupted state he had carefully constructed for her" (128). This merging of Fleda's identity with the landscape prefigures his own final silence.

Eventually he loses himself in the landscape he has created, drawn in by the power of the whirlpool and his desire to "submerge. To place oneself below and lose character, identity, inside another element" (80), to substitute the water of the whirlpool for "the world above ... He would swim there and take the world above with him, if necessary" (81). At the end he sees the whirlpool everywhere, "'not only down there' ... Patrick moved his head towards the bank, 'it's also up here.' He waved his other hand vaguely somewhere above his head. 'I've been to the observatory in Ottawa and I've seen it'" (177). In mistaking the actual for the imaginative and metaphoric and in choosing what he thinks is neutrality (222), he enters the whirlpool and drowns. He has done precisely what he attempted not to do, and what the new world demands – he has blurred the boundaries of ordering categories:

"Keep the sequence of fear, of quest, of desire in logical order – compartmentalized and exact. Try not to bring one with you into the other. Do not confuse fear with desire, desire with quest, quest with fear. Otherwise the world scrambles, becomes unidentifiable, loses its recognizable context" (191–2). As the world scrambles, Patrick moves further and further out of context and into disorder, retreating from his home in Ottawa to his uncle's house on the Niagara frontier, in which he dreams of its reordered rooms and contents, and then to the edge of the river that borders the country: his move into the landscape signals the ultimate disorder, in which whirlpools *are* everywhere.

Patrick needs to understand the whirlpool as metaphor, not as physical phenomenon. Had he grasped the new world's nature as metaphoric construct, he might well have written its poetry and contributed to the making of cultural place. Instead, he approaches space both personally and literally: he equates Fleda with landscape and dies the death she has already dreamed for him (100). The Canadian landscape does not conform to his or to Browning's old world ideas of structure and control: like David, he requires the closure that is absent here. That need can only result not in the invention of new world discourse but in a perception of the new world as nightmare – forest fires, whirlpools – and in the silence of the new world poet.

The reactions of the women in the novel to the demands of the new world are significantly different from the men's. Their discourses – Fleda's diary, Maud's book of floaters – are already at some remove from the more traditional forms the men use, and their lives less conventional: Urquhart suggests that adaptability is demanded by the new world and implies that women may be particularly well suited to meet that demand because, by necessity, their lives have taught them that skill. In refusing traditional female roles and canonized literary forms, Fleda and Maud not only make their lives possible in their own terms but enable the imaginative transformation of the new world and a profound articulation of cultural place.

Fleda moves out of the confining patterns of female behaviour by refusing her expected roles of wife and mother: "She wouldn't ever want to be Patmore's wife, Patmore's angel. Not now, not ever" (54). Refusing to be anyone's angel, she leaves the house she and David once lived in, moves out of the dark rooms in town to live in the tent above the whirlpool, then cuts her hair and wears men's clothing. In a climactic scene she counterpoints David's and Patrick's discussion of the theoretical dimension of war by humming and then singing hymns while marching slowly around them. She turns their lack of response against them and "stop[s], at that moment, responding to either one of them" (212). Her singing of hymns, not unlike Maud's compulsive piano-playing the night her husband and his parents die, withdraws power from the men and releases Fleda from the poetical and conventional confines implied by the text's old world Browning frame; thus she is released from her textual confines as well. She moves from spoken language to song to silence, refusing Laura Secord's example – "*It wasn't the message that was important. It was the walk. The journey. Setting forth*" (219) – and transcends the narrative, moving into a fiction of her own making where neither reader nor author can follow. She ceases to be merely the reader of other people's writing or the body that both David and Patrick attempt to use as material for their own work.

The violence of that appropriation and silencing is explicit. Patrick erases her entirely by making her into landscape; David replays the woman-as-landscape motif by using her as the battlefield where he nightly re-enacts his war, with himself as hero and victor: "He made love, for all his kindness, like a man fighting a short, intense battle, a battle that he always won. She lay passively beneath him like a town surprised by an invasion of enemy troops. Afterwards, he fell asleep almost immediately, like a man overcome by battle fatigue" (53). She refuses the passive role and insists on acting, but not on narrative closure: "Fleda had set her little boats adrift and had walked away. She followed Laura Secord's route but she carried with her no deep messages" (234). The fact that her action takes her into the landscape and beyond the reach of reader and text is crucial: in that metaphoric act she comes to terms with the physicality of the new world as well as with its discursive nature. Her body is *not* found, in either the whirlpool or the bush, although of course David believes it will be. She can make the transition into landscape in a way that Patrick cannot because she has understood the nature of discourse here. Her new world existence is only somewhat analogous to Jeremy's in *Gone Indian*. Her departure is not an escape, as Jeremy's in some ways is; she leaves nothing behind that can be transcribed into text or any form of closure. *Fleda takes her diary with her* – this is the *beginning* of the writing of the new world, not the end.

Maud similarly shows her ability not simply to survive but to flourish in the new world. One of the duties of her undertaking business, which she takes over after her husband's death, is the disposal of the fragments of corpses turned up by the river. Maud saves and records the artifacts of the battle with the river, but although her notebook entries are carefully detailed and dated, they betray a fundamental lack of order:

Body of a Man Found at Maid of the Mist Landing July 3rd, 1889
Then, after pausing to refill her pen, she continued:
  Dark grey hair
  Narrow leather belt
  Laundry mark D.N.
  Heavy fleece-lined underdrawers
  Corduroy pants
  Shoe about number 9, plain without toe caps
  Fleece-lined undershirt with marker (D.N.)
  Blue polka dot handkerchief
  Half a packet of Fashion smoking tobacco
  Bone pipe stem with silver funnel
  Also a Peterson pipe
  25 cents Canadian and 10 cents American
  Good teeth
  About 5 ft. 10 inches in height   (95)

Her activity is parallel to David's. As he attempts to write new world history, she attempts to gather the individual artifacts that make up that history: she keeps his museum. She too expects artifacts to mean something, but their very randomness defeats her: "Who was this man, this D.N.? She would more than likely never know" (95). Enacting the role of archivist, Maud becomes the keeper of these memories (95), recording and tying the relics up in neat sacks in the hall closet, not for the unlikely claiming by a relative but for herself: to maintain order, to gather some sense out of the chaos of the deaths around her (165). She does to the floaters what society has tried to do to her: impose narrative coherence and closure. Women's roles are conflated for her in the image of the dead bride, the young woman who is married on her deathbed with her wedding gown lying on top of her and then put inside the gown to be buried, with her trousseau stuffed into the coffin with her (148–9). Maud has been bride and wife and is now widow – her skin is marked by the dye from her mourning clothes and her life is threatened as, blinded by her black veils, she walks in front of carriages and streetcars. By taking over her husband's family's business, Maud steps out of traditional women's roles; by realizing what the next stage could be for her, she refuses it: "Bride, wife, widow. She would not stop now" (149).

It is Maud's child who makes the inhabitation of the new world possible and who shows within the text the process that Fleda enacts by walking out of it. The child's unique perception of both world and language begins the formation and articulation of new world discourse. Maud displaces her personal and intellectual conflict over containment from the floaters to her autistic son. Just as she attempts to impose a coherent narrative on silent lives and deaths, she tries to reach her son through language: she obsessively names the objects around him and demands a verbal response. She does not at first realize that her apparent success is the beginning of a new ordering: the literal nonsense the child speaks is, metaphorically, profound. His use of language is within a system of meaning that is entirely new: he mimics voices, parrots his mother's speech, simultaneously narrates her actions and describes her feelings to her, and acts out the funerals he has overheard. In so doing and in his wordplay with Patrick he both demonstrates and breaks the rigid and arbitrary conventions language and text are expected to use, which originate in the old world and parallel its rigid cultural conventions. He also reclassifies the artifacts in the closet by property rather than by ownership. By reordering language and forcing those around him to completely rethink their systems of classification, he reorders the universe and performs an intellectual and discursive act that allows the imaginative inhabitation of the new world.

In his otherness the child is outside social expectations and within the discursive system that Patrick, the failed new world poet who has "found it difficult to speak at all" (69), is unable to find or use: "This child, these words, disconnected from their sources, began to astound Patrick, to set up ridiculous yet poetic associations ... The child's uttered nonsense was a revelation, not unlike the intoxicating leaps he had known himself to take, only once or twice, in the manipulation of language ... Suddenly, by virtue of its very randomness, the child's speech became profound" (111–12). He also turns the self-and-other relationship, which is so problematic for Patrick, on its head: "The boy pointed at Patrick and said the word 'I.' Then he pointed at himself and said the word 'you'"(188). His words work in another register as well – his "Oh, the man" and "swim" would explain Patrick's death to anyone who could understand the new ordering of language and processes of categorization that the new world demands. The essence of that new ordering is linked to a recognition of the discursive nature of the new world: the apprehension of language here, as in Watson's text, must be of both literal and metaphoric registers, and include the act of invention that precedes the inhabitation of the new world and the articulation of place.

The new world dialogue of the child and Patrick consists of silence and apparently random words. The child's new world vision, which opens up startling possibilities and revelations, is necessarily difficult to communicate in language and is another articulation of Watson's double hook. The text suggests that the child's discursive ability will be shared, but not with Patrick. Patrick does not fully understand that the child's speaking is within a new system of perception and understanding or that his own work will never reproduce this place in words: the new world disallows literal mimesis, and Patrick is incapable of any other. Patrick's ability to participate in or even see the new world is impaired by the conventional conditioning of the old, in which the new world registers only as chaos and nightmare. Such failure of understanding and imagination is fatal in this setting, silencing Patrick's poetry and causing his death. The dominant discourses of Patrick's and David's professions disintegrate.

As the men fall silent and the unusual child becomes the centre of the new world's discursive activity and meaning, the women enact its possibility. The epiphany that the child makes possible for Maud frees her from her obsession with the floaters and from the closed world she was being drawn into, to drown. As with the floaters, a sudden movement throws her out of that field of force to determine her own direction: "*Dislodge: to remove, turn out from position. Perhaps the knowledge comes at the moment of departure*" (176). Fleda's departure is similarly enabled by her separation from the force that draws the floaters and the men in and down. The women are able to release themselves from the confining structures of their marriages and patterns of behaviour imposed on them as nineteenth-century women; they are trapped neither in the endless circles in which their lives are set to run nor in the end-stopped patterns of the men. They can accommodate themselves to the contradictory conditions of the new world and make the whirlpool's circular motion both sustaining and enabling: "[Fleda] had broken out of the world of corners and into the organic in a way that even her beloved poets in their cottages and villas hadn't the power to do, and the acre had become her house. The acre and the whirlpool. Predictable flux, ..." (142). The inhabitation of the new world is not only freeing and empowering for Fleda and Maud but is essentially new. As Maud and Fleda, along with the child, reject old world hierarchies, they also reject Wordsworth's daffodils, Patrick's empty landscapes, and David's painless, bloodless fields of battle. What Patrick thinks is a joining with new world landscape is literally death by drowning, while the perimeter of David's world shrinks (231) as he loses his wife and his sense of order to the whirlpool: "It was as though McDougal's world were evaporating right before his eyes, cartwheeling vaguely away into another nationality, taking everything familiar with it" (229). The quilt speaks Urquhart's concern: to recognize the *newness* of the new world and its discursive organization, and the consequent necessity of different ways of using and understanding language, different ways of understanding self and place.

The old world frame of the inner text, Browning's death-day, points up again the conflict between ways of knowing that the new world provokes. Browning admits that his tidy and well-ordered life in Venice has been against the light of the artist – suntreader, eagle, shape-shifter – that he had never dared to be. In contrast to Shelley, whom he idealizes, he "had placed himself in the centre of some of the world's most exotic scenery and had then lived his life there with the regularity of a copy clerk" (11). Browning's world, like David's, shrinks. He knows early on what the ending will be, and that it will be soon: "He was pleased that he had prudently written his death poem ... It was the final poem of his last manuscript which was now, mercifully, at the printer's" (10). Searching for a suitable form of closure for his life and writing in the shadow of Shelley's violent death, he takes some comfort in knowing that his last trip too will be by water, to the cemetery island. The frame and inner text merge: Browning ponders Shelley's drowning; the sister and son hypothesize about Browning's last day; Maud dreams about her floaters. Both frame and inner text move from images of death and arrested disintegration (Bradbury 64) – the dead, floating bodies of Shelley, Browning, Patrick, and the floaters – to Shelley's "*Suntreader ... A moulted feather, an eagle feather*" (237), Maud's bright yellow dress, and Fleda's absent body. The images transfigure to make both stories one, to make history and reality and fiction inseparable: "In one sense the whirlpool was like memory; like obsession connected to memory, like history that stayed in one spot, moving nowhere and endlessly repeating itself" (49). Urquhart's point is that the new world's history cannot be an endless repetition of a pattern taken from elsewhere, that its poetry must not impose Browning's premature closure but put people into a landscape of pine trees: its special discourses must authentically enact and articulate the processes of cultural invention. The novel ends not with the closure demanded by Patrick and David and rejected by Fleda and Maud but with the transformation Fleda accomplished that allows the new world to determine and discover its own future: "*Little white vessels departing from the shore, set adrift on a long tour of the whirlpool. Like people, just like people. A complete revolution would be a long, long life. Not many are able to go the distance*" (60).

In Urquhart's terms, to go the distance is to recognize the implications of making and making sense of new world culture. Her novel figures the new world's discursive construction and its problematizing of reading, writing, and knowing the present and the past in this place. The echo of Richardson in Urquhart's return to his historical terrain and the War of 1812 is fitting: the position on the western frontier during a period requiring political and ideological definition and commitment constitutes the potentially freeing or disabling anxiety and displacement that Kroetsch focuses precisely in his attention to the border metaphor. Urquhart covers the huge conceptual distance from the threatening forest that surrounds Richardson, the shifting farmyards and fences of Grove's prairie, the nothingness on the other side of Watson's hill, and the equivocal future existence of Kroetsch's protagonist. She claims not simply that the recognition of the discursive nature of the new world may make possible continued existence here, but that such a recognition is the only guarantor of new world culture. Silence is still a real presence in this text, but Fleda's chosen and informed decision not to be heard is far different from the silences of annihilation and anxiety we have seen earlier. *The Whirlpool*'s exploration of various forms of new world writing demonstrates the process by which the cultural narrative occurs; in particular, its historiographic and metafictional inquiries bring into focus the new world's rhetorical construction, as well as the crippling lack of solid, stable, sustaining discursive practices from which Richardson and others have suffered.

Urquhart does not look to the "hill country of England ... or gentle undulations of the Tuscan countryside, [which] had nothing to do with this" (31) as the model to which the Canadian place must accommodate itself, but uses instead the figure of the landscape's contradiction – the whirlpool – to explore perception, imagination, and history while contextualizing those processes in the new world. She also reorders the conceptual frame in which power is determined (Ashcroft, Griffiths, Tiffin 115) and refuses the conventional strategies of closure and completion, which are inappropriate and ineffective here. Urquhart shows the invention of a cultural process that demands recognition of the collusion of literary and historical discourses and of their own status as human constructs. In so doing she enacts the construction of the new world's way of speaking and knowing, exhibits a historical and cultural consciousness of the new world's discursive construction, and comments significantly on writing itself. She also writes the new world.

CHAPTER SEVEN

Conclusion: Imagining Culture

In a discussion of African and European writing James Snead observes that "the unclarity about the real nature of 'African' or 'European' writing participates in a more general quandary over the indefatigable, yet ultimately indefinable word 'nation'" (231). We could substitute Canadian for African and European in this configuration: it is generally acknowledged that the Canadian nation currently exists in a condition of unclarity and general quandary. That this quandary on the level of political and ideological authority has its correlative in a historical unclarity regarding the status and interpretation of its cultural products should pose no surprise to theorists of nation or of national cultures.

The current difficulty of the Canadian nation in defining an apparatus of state power has its roots, as we know, in the historical presence of the two founding nations – added to that is the more recent melting of the cultural mosaic under the pressure of an ever-enlarging group of contending ethnicities[1] – and the perpetual agony of language in this country. In the light of Benedict Anderson's linkage of the great sacral cultures with sacred language and written script (12ff.), it is not unreasonable to suspect an association between language and a secular culture: how a community imagines itself is linked to how it speaks and thinks about itself. If the imagining has occurred within the culture, or cultural/linguistic groups within the nation, then the task causing difficulty in Canada is the accompanying creation of what Ernest Gellner calls the political shell (17). The fact that the limits of these language and culture groups are not precise within either the designation of anglophone Canada, a boundary observed here, or even the biographies of the writers discussed here may in itself make an interesting point about the modern nation-state and cultural difference: Richardson's Scots ancestry is most likely supplemented by native Ottawa; the fluidity of Grove's national designations is legendary; Watson is born in Canada as a British subject of Irish origin and achieves Canadian citizenship simply by being here; Kroetsch locates one branch of his ancestry in eastern Canada and another in Germany, and earns his reputation as a Canadian writer while enacting the emigrant experience; Urquhart's Irish ancestry on one side of her family is uneasily balanced by lines of descent from the English oppressor on the other. In a culture such as Canada's, with ethnic and national origins both increasingly differentiated and distant in time and space, it may well appear that we have returned full circle to the question posed by Ernest Renan more than a century ago – what is a nation?[2]

The ways in which Benedict Anderson, Homi Bhabha, and Timothy Brennan discuss nation, narrative, and cultural fictions are of some help in thinking about Canada in this context; I would like briefly to set some of their ideas into relationship with the work here. The nation-centredness of the post-colonial world is noted by Brennan, who suggests that cultural study, specifically the study of imaginative literature, may well prove useful for understanding that condition (47). Bhabha puts the terms of the inquiry like this: "If the ambivalent figure of the nation is a problem of its transitional history, its conceptual indeterminacy, its wavering between vocabularies, then what effect does this have on narratives and discourses that signify a sense of 'nationness'?" ("Narrating" 2) If the figure of the nation is ambivalent, then the attempts to define and explore its cultural significance through a cultural product – its narrative – are doubly so, and put into question our configuration of national literature/s. Anderson's well-known definition of the modern nation is this: "it is an imagined political community ... *imagined* because the members of even the smallest nation will never know most of their fellow-members, meet them, or even hear of them, yet in the minds of each lives the image of their communion ... it is imagined as a *community* because, regardless of the actual inequality and exploitation that may prevail in each, the nation is always conceived as a deep, horizontal comradeship" (6–7). Anderson formulates nationality as a way of linking fraternity, power, and time in reaction to changes in the conception of sacred language, the perceived divinity of monarchs, and temporality (36); simultaneous with these changes in cultural conceptions is the imagining of a sociological landscape. The Canadian preoccupation with the socio-logical landscape – demonstrated in the obsession with ideological and state apparatus – points up the sense of a lack of absolute beginnings, an experience not unique among post-colonial cultures or modern nation-states, and returns us to the questions of cultural origins and imagining touched on earlier.

In the Introduction I discussed the particular relationship between a new culture and its history, a relationship formulated variously by Bhabha and Anderson,[3] and in this way by Snead: "from the loss of absolute beginnings the need for arbitrary begin-nings flows" (234). Colin Partridge suggests that the need for those arbitrary beginnings is met in a new culture by its creation of myth and metaphor, which he describes as the home-made legend that will come to shape the culture's perceptions of its past (18). This home-made legend is suggestive of Bhabha's notion that the culture is the creator of its own origins and continued existence – that in narrating itself the imagined community creates itself (6) – and of Brennan's position that nations are imaginary constructs that depend for their existence on an apparatus of cultural fictions in which imaginative literature plays a decisive role (49). If we agree with Brennan that literary myth is complicit in the creation of nations (49), we may also agree that in Canada the cultural fiction or national narrative has been constructed largely on the level of sociological landscape, a preoccupation of the Canadian political, educational, and cultural infrastructures in both centuries of the nation's existence.

In contrast, the cultural fiction that I understand Richardson, Grove, Watson, Kroetsch, and Urquhart to be imagining is a met-aphoric landscape. In Bhabha's understanding of cultural narrative, metaphor transfers the meaning of home and belonging across the distances and cultural differences that span the imagined commu-nity of the nation-state ("DissemiNation" 291); he suggests that the metaphoricity of the peoples of imagined communities "requires a kind of doubleness in writing; a temporality of representation that moves between cultural formations and social processes without a 'centred' causal logic" (293). The ambivalence and liminality of the modern nation-state extends to its cultural representation; Canada's nationness as well as its cultural fictions exist in this condition:

"that large and liminal image of the nation ... is a particular ambivalence that haunts the idea of the nation, the language of those who write of it and the lives of those who live it" ("Narrating" 1). We have seen here the haunting of language and imagination that attends the creation of origins, belonging, and metaphor out of "the perplexity of living and writing the nation" ("DissemiNation" 311) and the new world, and of imagining culture.

Notes

CHAPTER ONE: INTRODUCTION

1 See also, for example, Spivak, Bhabha, and Brotherson on the question of the other.
2 Spivak has produced a complex body of work, some of which is relevant to this topic. See the Bibliography.
3 These are the new names Columbus chose for the first islands he encountered.
4 O'Gorman would agree with Sheila Watson that words mean.
5 See Brotherson and Greenblatt on the literacy of the Americas' indigenous peoples.
6 This polemic is traced by Gerbi.
7 See Gerbi (28–9) and Carter (42–52) for discussion of this issue.
8 This is an admittedly brief account of post-colonial thought. See the Bibliography for further reading.
9 Slemon's theorizing of the second world is part of the complex argument he makes in "Unsettling the Empire."
10 The fact of francophone Canada doubles the country's neither/nor conditions; some aspects of my argument here would apply to French Canada's culture and literature, and some would not.
11 I discuss Richardson as if he were of European descent only, which is how he identified himself during his lifetime. Some critics claim his Indian ancestry; see chapter 2.
12 Urquhart's husband's grandmother kept a book of floaters found in the Niagara River. The published text is Cruikshank's *Whirlpool Heights*. See notes to chapter 6.

CHAPTER TWO: JOHN RICHARDSON

1 I use Richardson's spelling of Ponteac, Michillimackinac, and Sinclair River.

2 Dennis Duffy discusses the historical conditions of the frontier on which Richardson lived, and which informed his sense of British North America. See "John Richardson's Dream World," 3–6.

3 The position of the speaking subject bears some scrutiny in Richardson's work. *Frascati's*, the second of his European novels and written immediately before *Wacousta*, is a travel narrative in the first person and, as such, interesting preparation for his new world work.

4 For a discussion of Richardson and Scott, see Richards, "Nineteenth-Century Scottish and Canadian Fiction," in Chew, ed., *Revisions of Canadian Literature*.

5 These critics include Moss, *Sex and Violence in the Canadian Novel*, 88–90; Lecker, "Patterns of Deception in *Wacousta*," 77–85; and Hurley, "*Wacousta*: The Borders of Nightmare."

6 The situation is a milder and more sentimental version of a triangular relationship in *The Monk Knight of St. John*.

7 He may also be saying much about himself: many critics believe that his maternal grandmother was an Ottawa Indian, although debate continues on the point. Certainly if he was part Ottawa, the whole intercultural dynamic in this novel, as well as in his other new world works, is even more complex.

   Liaisons and marriages between native women and white traders and settlers were not uncommon, although Richardson would seem to deny that possibility, at least to someone of Frederick's class.

8 This is not because Richardson is sensitive or hesitant: rape figures prominently in *The Monk Knight* and *Westbrook*.

9 Hurley, "The Borders of Nightmare," 65. Hurley further identifies the numerous parallels in plot and character.

10 See the discussion of the other in the Introduction.

11 The pressure on different cultural groups is more complex in Richardson's historical context than he presents it here. See Duffy, "Dream World."

12 Robertson, writing about prairie immigrant literature, defines exile as the sense of existing in two worlds, the physical here, the mental or ghostly there; alien is being lost between two cultures, part of each residing in oneself. "My Own Country," 79.

13 Harrison, "The Beginnings of Prairie Fiction," 176. See also Harrison's *Unnamed Country*, particularly chap. 1. McGregor argues a similar point in *The Wacousta Syndrome*: that conventionalizing the landscape not only allows the convention to shape the viewer's response and limits literary expression but also impairs the ability to come to terms with the actual environment (33–6).

14 I use the term in the Hartzian sense; see the works of Louis Hartz listed in the Bibliography.

15 Duffy, "Major John Richardson," in *Gardens, Covenants, Exiles,* 51–3. Duffy argues further that the observer stance leads him into voyeurism, with its spying and masking, as he wishes to participate but is stopped by his fear of the act. This is the method of detachment Richardson usually employs when dealing with sex or violence.

16 Robertson identifies an intermediate stage in the move from the old world to the new, which he calls the middle passage: "the psychic shift from one culture to another involves a middle period of 'wandering between two worlds.'" "My Own Country," 78.

CHAPTER THREE:
FREDERICK PHILIP GROVE

1 The continuing research of Spettigue and Hjartarson, the identification of Elsa as the Baroness Elsa von-Freytag Loringhoven, and the publication of the Baroness's autobiography mean that more and more of Grove's two lives are becoming known.

2 Healy, "Grove and the Matter of Germany," 170–87. Reprinted in Hjartarson, ed., *A Stranger to My Time*, 89–106.

3 Spettigue's research shows that Grove's account of Grove's European past is different from Greve's life in Europe. See Spettigue, *FPG: The European Years*. We are given an idea of what he may have left behind in De Vore's "The Backgrounds of *Nightwood*: Robin, Felix, and Nora," 71–90. De Vore claims that Felix Paul Greve was the model for Baron Felix Volokbein in *Nightwood* and identifies Greve's Elsa as Baroness Elsa von-Freytag Loringhoven, with whom he lived for years in Europe, upon whom he based *Fanny Essler*, and whom he eventually deserted, De Vore says, in Kentucky. In *Nightwood* the character of Felix is obsessed with history – or its absence – and his fraudulent aristocratic past. Hjartarson discusses De Vore's article along with his own research on

Barnes's papers in "Of Greve, Grove, and Other Strangers," in Hjartarson, ed., *A Stranger to My Time*, 269–84. See also Scobie's discussion of the search for Grove's origins within the context of Canadian literature in *Signature Event Cantext*, 138–44. See also Spettigue, "Felix, Elsa, André Gide and Others," and *Baroness Elsa*, ed. Spettigue and Hjartarson.

4 Grove's first letter to Isaak Warkentin in 1913 is in German, and he apparently began *Settlers of the Marsh* in German. With these exceptions, however, the evidence suggests that in his literary life in North America he used English. He also denied his German nationality, which suggests that he would have avoided drawing attention to himself by using the language.

5 See Giltrow, "Grove in Search of an Audience."

6 "Rebels All" may be early in Grove's Canadian writing life: for a discussion of its possible date, see Hjartarson, ed., *A Stranger to My Time*, 67.

7 See Spettigue, *FPG*, 190–1, and "Felix, Elsa, André Gide and Others"; and Gide's *Conversation avec un Allemand* and *Journals*, discussed in Spettigue, *FPG*, 119–31. It would seem that whatever relationship did exist was professional rather than personal.

8 My ideas on autobiography here are indebted to Eakin, *Fictions in Autobiography*.

9 This is with the exception of the children's book he wrote with his son in mind, *The Adventures of Leonard Broadus*.

10 Spettigue lists numerous coincidences of names, ages, and events in Grove's and Greve's writing and in the evidence of Greve's real life and the life-history Grove constructs. Greve/Grove used fragments of truth, transposed in various fashions but bearing a relation to his actual experience: Greve's father is Carl Eduard; Fanny's last lover is Friedrich Carl Reelen; one of Greve's pseudonyms is Friedrich Carl Gerden. In *The Master Mason's House* Susie Ihle's mother is named Bertha and is the same age in the novel when her marriage is breaking up as is Bertha Reichentrog Greve in similar circumstances. Greve's and Grove's birthdays are both 14 February, but Greve is born in 1879 instead of 1873, making the Canadian Grove younger than he claimed to be. The European travels did occur, but during and after his university years instead of his childhood. Uncle Jacobsen, the boarding-house in Hamburg, his parents' separation, the absence/death of sister(s), the purported nationalities

(Swedish, Russian, German), the distant or absent authoritarian father-figures are all true in some form, and turn up repeatedly in various forms in his writing. A novel titled *Felix Powell's Career* was apparently destroyed by Mrs Grove or on her instructions. For further details, see Spettigue's FPG, especially "Framing An Auto-biography," 169–96.

11 In the manuscript copybook of *Our Daily Bread* Grove has much more completely developed the relationship between John and Martha Elliot. Elliot has a more healthy and balanced relationship with his wife, both emotionally and rationally: they show each other personal, emotional warmth, and she answers his questions about "the problem of his age–scepticism" with an admonition to faith. Elliot is much more able to communicate.

12 Anthony Riley discusses the parallels between elements of *Fanny Essler* and what we know of Greve's life in "The Case of Greve/ Grove," in Riedel, ed., *The Old World and the New*, 48. See also Hjartarson, "Of Greve, Grove, and Other Strangers."

13 Several critics discuss various aspects of Grove's treatment of and attitude towards women in his German and Canadian novels. See Blodgett, "Alias Grove," in *Configuration*, abr. and rev. as "Ersatz Feminism in FPG's German Novels," in Hjartarson, ed., *A Stranger to My Time*; McMullen, "Women in Grove's Novels"; McKenna, "As They Really Were"; Riley and Spettigue, Introduction to *Fanny Essler*; Potvin, "'The Eternal Feminine' and the Clothing Motif in Grove's Fiction."

14 The genres he used seem further mixed if we consider his published and unpublished essays. In particular, the essays he delivered pub-licly on his speaking tours on the topics of Canadian nationhood and immigration and the clash of the values of Europe and Amer-ica are an interesting counterpart to the ideas about the new world individual and society in his fiction. See "Nationhood," in *It Needs To Be Said*, and "Canadians Old and New" and "Assimilation," in *A Stranger to My Time*. See also Padolsky's discussion of Grove's ideas, those essays, and the historical and political context: "Grove's 'Nationhood' and the European Immigrant." Padolsky briefly discusses Grove's expression of those ideas in his fiction in his introduction to the first publication of Grove's "Foreigners." Craig discusses this topic as well: "F.P. Grove and the 'Alien' Immi-gration in the West."

CHAPTER FOUR: SHEILA WATSON

1 Most critics ignore or justify thematically or symbolically the fact that the action in this novel is initiated by the murder of a woman by her son. The exceptions are Davidson's "*The Double Hook*'s Double Hook" and Rooke's "Women of *The Double Hook*." Grace also discusses Mrs Potter as something more than an image of sterility and evil in a chapter on Watson in *Regression and Apocalypse*, 200–3. See also Scobie's discussion of the desire of/for the absent father in *The Double Hook* in *Signature Event Cantext*, 51–4.

2 Grace points out that one aspect of the condition of the figures in the novel is their lack of "a particularizing past," that "they exist primarily in a presentness that oppresses and threatens to overwhelm them." Grace makes the further point that "this minimalizing of context, consciousness, and temporal perspective serves to dehumanize and abstract these figures" (198), which is consistent with her argument relating Watson to abstract expressionism. It is also consistent with my arguing of the new world's discursive construction. For a further discussion of the "spareness and immediacy that come to characters when they have no alternative but to *be* in their time and place" as well as the "series of decisions by means of which Sheila Watson wrote *The Double Hook*," see Flahiff's 1984 introduction to *The Double Hook*.

3 See Grace's discussion of *The Double Hook* in the context of abstract expressionism in *Regression and Apocalypse*, 185–209.

4 *Five Stories*, 71–6. See Neuman, "Sheila Watson," *Profiles in Canadian Literature*, 45–52. Scobie also discusses "And the Four Animals" and argues that it stands as an introduction or prologue to *The Double Hook* in *Sheila Watson and Her Works*, 18–29.

CHAPTER FIVE: ROBERT KROETSCH

1 Davidson discusses the relationships between Jeremy, Madham, and Sunderman in some detail in "Will the Real R. Mark Madham Please Stand Up."

CHAPTER SIX: JANE URQUHART

1 The undertaker's widow who recorded the floaters was the author's husband's grandmother; the military historian's wife was Julia

Cruikshank, whose *Whirlpool Heights: The Dream-House on the Niagara River* was published in 1915. Urquhart says that Archibald Lampman is her model for Patrick because he died in 1889, as did Browning. See my paper on Cruikshank, "The Woman in the Text."

CHAPTER SEVEN: CONCLUSION

1 See Healy, "The Melting of the Mosaic."
2 Renan's essay appears in Bhabha, *Nation and Narration,* 8–22; see also Anderson, *Imagined Communities,* chap. 6, "Official Nationalism and Imperialism," 83–112.
3 Bhabha is quoted by Tiffin in "Counter-Discourse," 21; see also Anderson, *Imagined Communities,* 204.

Bibliography

PRIMARY SOURCES

Grove, Frederick Philip. Manuscript copybook of *Our Daily Bread*. In the Department of Archives and Special Collections, Elizabeth Dafoe Library, University of Manitoba.

SECONDARY SOURCES

Anderson, Benedict. *Imagined Communities: Reflections on the Origin and Spread of Nationalism*. Rev. ed. London and New York: Verso 1991.

Ashcroft, Bill, Gareth Griffiths, and Helen Tiffin. *The Empire Writes Back: Theory and Practice in Post-colonial Literatures*. London, New York: Routledge 1989.

Ball, John Clement. "The Carnival of Babel: The Construction of Voice in Robert Kroetsch's 'Out West' Triptych." *Essays on Canadian Writing* 39, 1 (1989): 1–22.

Barker, Francis, Peter Hulme, Margaret Iversen, and Diana Loxley, eds. *Europe and Its Others*. Colchester: University of Essex 1985.

Beasley, David. *The Canadian Don Quixote: The Life and Works of Major John Richardson, Canada's First Novelist*. Erin: Porcupine's Quill 1977.

Berger, Peter L., and Thomas Luckmann. *The Social Construction of Reality: A Treatise in the Sociology of Knowledge*. New York: Anchor 1967.

Berkhofer, Robert F., Jr. *The White Man's Indian: Images of the American Indian from Columbus to the Present*. New York: Alfred A. Knopf 1978.

Bhabha, Homi. "Of Mimicy and Men: The Ambivalence of Colonial Discourse." *October* 28 (1984): 125–33.

- "Signs Taken for Wonders: Questions of Ambivalence and Authority under a Tree outside Delhi, May 1817." *Critical Inquiry* 21, 1 (1985): 144–65.
- "The Other Question: Difference, Discrimination and the Discourse of Colonialism." In *Literature, Politics and Theory.* Ed. Francis Barker et al. London and New York: Methuen 1986.
- "Introduction: Narrating the Nation." In Bhaba, ed., *Nation and Narration.* 1–7.
- "DissemiNation: Time, Narrative, and the Margins of the Modern Nation." In Bhaba, ed., *Nation and Narration.* 291–322.
- ed. *Nation and Narration.* London and New York: Routledge 1990.

Blodgett, E.D. "*Alias* Grove: Variations in Disguise." *Configuration: Essays on the Canadian Literatures.* Toronto: ECW 1982. 112–53. Rev. as "Ersatz Feminism in F.P. Grove's German Novels." In *A Stranger to My Time.* Ed. Paul Hjartarson. Edmonton: NeWest 1986. 21–46.
- "Gone West to Geometry's Country." In Blodgett, *Configuration.* 187–218.
- "European Theory and Canadian Criticism." *Zeitschrift der Gesellschaft fur Kanada-Studien* 6, 2 (1986): 5–15.

Bowering, George. "Sheila Watson, Trickster." *The Mask in Place: Essays on Fiction in North America.* Winnipeg: Turnstone 1982. 97–111.

Bradbury, Patricia. "Jane Urquhart's Short Stories in the Landscape of the Poet." *Quill & Quire* 53, 7 (1987): 64–5.

Brennan, Timothy. "The National Longing for Form." In *Nation and Narration.* Ed. Homi Bhabha. London and New York: Routledge 1990. 44–70.

Brotherson, Gordon. "Towards a Grammatology of America: Lévi-Strauss, Derrida, and the Native New World Text." In *Europe and Its Others.* Ed. Francis Barker et al. Colchester: University of Essex 1985. 61–77.

Canary, Robert H., and Henry Kozicki, eds. *The Writing of History: Literary Form and Historical Understanding.* Madison, Wisc.: University of Wisconsin Press 1978.

Carter, Paul. *The Road to Botany Bay: An Exploration of Landscape and History.* Chicago: University of Chicago Press 1987.

Chew, Shirley, ed. *Re-visions of Canadian Literature.* Leeds: University of Leeds 1984.

Chiapelli, Fredi, Michael J.B. Allen, and Robert E. Benson, eds. *First Images of America: The Impact of the New World on the Old.* 2 vols. Berkeley, Los Angeles, London: University of California Press 1976.

Craig, Terrence L. "F.P. Grove and the 'Alien' Immigration in the West." *Journal of Canadian Studies* 20, 2 (1985): 92–100.

Cruikshank, Julia. *Whirlpool Heights: The Dream-House on the Niagara River*. London: George Allen and Unwin 1915.

Davey, Frank, and bp Nichol, eds. *Robert Kroetsch: Essays. Open Letter* 5, 4 (1983).

Davidson, Arnold E. "Will the Real R. Mark Madham Please Stand Up: A Note on Robert Kroetsch's *Gone Indian*." *Studies in Canadian Literature* 5, 3 (1980): 135–9.

– "*The Double Hook*'s Double Hooks." *Canadian Literature* 116 (1988): 29–41.

De Vore, Lynn. "The Backgrounds of *Nightwood*: Robin, Felix, and Nora." *Journal of Modern Literature* 10, 1 (1983): 71–90.

Duffy, Dennis. "Major John Richardson: The Loyalist in Disguise." *Gardens, Covenants, Exiles: Loyalism in the Literature of Upper Canada/Ontario*. Toronto, Buffalo, London: University of Toronto Press 1982. 44–54.

– "John Richardson's Dream World." ECW 47 (1992): 1–25.

Eakin, John Paul. *Fictions in Autobiography: Studies in the Art of Self-Invention*. Princeton: Princeton University Press 1985.

Elliott, J.H. *The Old World and the New 1492–1650*. Cambridge: Cambridge University Press 1970.

Flahiff, F.T. Introduction to *The Double Hook*. 1959. Toronto: McClelland and Stewart 1966. Introduction © 1984.

Foucault, Michel. *The Archaeology of Knowledge*. 1969. Trans. A.M. Sheridan Smith. London: Tavistock 1974.

Franklin, Wayne. *Discoverers, Explorers, Settlers: The Diligent Writers of Early America*. Chicago: University of Chicago Press 1979.

Gellner, Ernest. *Culture, Identity, and Politics*. Cambridge: Cambridge University Press 1987.

Gerbi, Antonio. *The Dispute of the New World: The History of a Polemic, 1750–1900*. 1955. Trans. J. Moyle. Pittsburgh: University of Pittsburgh Press 1973.

Giltrow, Janet. "Grove in Search of an Audience." *Canadian Literature* 90 (1981): 92–107.

Godard, Barbara. "'Between One Cliché and Another': Language in *The Double Hook*." *Studies in Canadian Literature* 3, 2 (1978): 149–65.

Goldie, Terry. *Fear and Temptation: The Image of the Indigene in Canadian, Australian, and New Zealand Literatures*. Kingston, Montreal, London: McGill-Queen's University Press 1989.

Grace, Sherrill E. *Regression and Apocalypse: Studies in North American Literary Expressionism*. Toronto, Buffalo, London: University of Toronto Press 1989.

Grant, George. *Technology and Empire: Perspectives on North America*. Toronto: Anansi 1969.

Greenblatt, Stephen J. "Learning to Curse: Aspects of Linguistic Colonialism in the Sixteenth Century." In *First Images of America: The Impact of the New World on the Old*. Ed. Fredi Chiappelli, Michael J.B. Allen, and Robert L. Benson. 2 vols. Berkeley, Los Angeles, London: University of California Press 1976. 2:561–80.

– *Marvellous Possessions: The Wonder of the New World*. Chicago: University of Chicago Press 1991.

Grove, Frederick Philip. *Fanny Essler*. 1905. 2 vols. Trans. Christine Helmers, A.W. Riley, and Douglas O. Spettigue. Ed. and intro. A.W. Riley and Douglas O. Spettigue. Toronto: Oberon 1984.

– *The Master Mason's House*. 1906. Trans. Paul P. Gubbins. Ed. A.W. Riley and Douglas O. Spettigue. Ottawa: Oberon 1976.

– *Over Prairie Trails*. 1922. Rpr Toronto: McClelland and Stewart 1970.

– *Settlers of the Marsh*. 1925. Rpr Toronto: McClelland and Stewart 1965.

– *A Search for America: The Odyssey of an Immigrant*. 1927. Rpr Toronto: McClelland and Stewart 1971.

– "Canadians Old and New." 1927. Rpr in *A Stranger to My Time*. Ed. Paul Hjartarson. Edmonton: NeWest 1986. 169–76.

– *Our Daily Bread*. 1928. Rpr Toronto: McClelland and Stewart 1975.

– *It Needs To Be Said*. 1929. Rpr ed. and intro. W.J. Keith. Ottawa: Tecumseh Press 1982.

– "Apologia Pro Vita et Opera Suo." 1931. Rpr in *A Stranger to My Time*. Ed. Paul Hjartarson. Edmonton: NeWest 1986. 191–8.

– *Fruits of the Earth*. 1933. Rpr Toronto: McClelland and Stewart 1965.

– *The Genesis of Grove's The Adventures of Leonard Broadus*. 1940. Rpr ed. Mary Rubio. Guelph: Canadian Children's Press 1983.

– *The Master of the Mill*. 1944. Rpr Toronto: McClelland and Stewart 1967.

– *In Search of Myself*. 1946. Rpr Toronto: McClelland and Stewart 1974.

– "Rebels All: Of the Interpretation of Individual Life." In *A Stranger to My Time*. Ed. Paul Hjartson. Edmonton: NeWest 1986. 67–82.

Harrison, Dick. "The Beginnings of Prairie Fiction." *Journal of Canadian Fiction* 4, 1 (1975): 159–77.

– *Unnamed Country: The Struggle for a Canadian Prairie Fiction*. Edmonton: University of Alberta Press 1977.

Hartz, Louis. *The Founding of New Societies: Studies in the History of the United States, Latin America, South Africa, Canada, and Australia.* New York: Harcourt Brace and World 1964.

– "Violence and Legality in the Fragment Cultures." *Canadian Historical Review* 50, 2 (1969): 123–40.

Healy, J.J. "Grove and the Matter of Germany: The Warkentin Letters and the Art of Liminal Disengagement." *Studies in Canadian Literature* 6, 1 (1981): 170–87. Rpr in *A Stranger to My Time.* Ed. Paul Hjartarson. Edmonton: NeWest 1986. 89–106.

– "Literature, Power and the Refusals of Big Bear: Reflections on the Treatment of the Indian and of the Aborigine." In *Australian / Canadian Literatures in English*: *Comparative Perspectives.* Ed. Russell McDougall and Gillian Whitlock. Melbourne: Methuen Australia 1987.

– "The Melting of the Mosaic: Landscape, Power and Ethnicity in Post-Confederation Canada." In Jean Burnet, Danielle Juteau, et al., eds. *Migration and the Transformation of Cultures.* Toronto: Multicultural History Society of Ontario 1992. 55–90.

Hjartarson, Paul. "Of Greve, Grove, and Other Strangers: The Autobiography of Baroness Elsa von Freytag-Loringhoven." In Hjartarson, ed., *A Stranger to My Time.* 269–84.

– *A Stranger to My Time: Essays by and about Frederick Philip Grove.* Edmonton: NeWest 1986.

Hjartarson, Paul, and Douglas Spettigue, eds. *Baroness Elsa.* Toronto: Oberon 1992.

Hulme, Peter. *Colonial Encounters: Europe and the Native Caribbean, 1492–1797.* London and New York: Methuen 1986.

Hurley, Michael. "*Wacousta*: The Borders of Nightmare." In *Beginnings: A Critical Anthology.* Ed. John Moss. Toronto: New Canada Publications 1980. 60–9.

Hutcheon, Linda. "Circling the Downspout of Empire." *Ariel* 20, 4 (1989): 149–75.

– *Splitting Images.* Toronto and Oxford: Oxford University Press 1991.

Kroetsch, Robert. *The Studhorse Man.* 1970. Rpr Markham: PaperJacks 1977.

– "The Canadian Writer and the American Literary Tradition." *English Quarterly* 4, 2 (1971). Rpr in *The Lovely Treachery of Words.* Toronto: Oxford 1989. 53–7.

– *Gone Indian.* Toronto: New Press 1973.

– Introduction to *Boundary* 2 3, 1 (1974): 1–2.

– "Unhiding the Hidden." *Journal of Canadian Fiction* 3, 3 (1974). Rpr in *The Lovely Treachery of Words.* Toronto: Oxford 1989. 58–63.

- "FPG: The Finding." *The Stone Hammer Poems: 1960–1975*. Nanaimo, BC: Oolichan 1975. 46–7.
- "The Fear of Women in Prairie Fiction: An Erotics of Space." In *Crossing Frontiers: Papers in American and Canadian Western Literature*. Ed. Dick Harrison. Edmonton: University of Alberta Press 1979. Rpr in *The Lovely Treachery of Words*. Toronto: Oxford 1989. 73–83.
- "The Exploding Porcupine." In *Violence in the Canadian Novel since 1960*. Ed. Terry Goldie and Virginia Harger-Grinling. St John's: Memorial University of Newfoundland 1980. Rpr in *The Lovely Treachery of Words*. Toronto: Oxford 1989. 108–16.
- "On Being an Alberta Writer." In *The New Provinces: Alberta and Saskatchewan, 1905–1980*. Ed. Howard Palmer and Donald Smith. Vancouver: Tantalus 1980. Rpr in *Robert Kroetsch: Essays*. Ed. Frank Davey and bp Nichol. *Open Letter* 5, 4 (1983): 69–80.
- *The Lovely Treachery of Words: Essays Selected and New*. Toronto: Oxford 1989.
- "No Name Is My Name." In *The Lovely Treachery of Words*. Toronto: Oxford 1989. 41–52.
- "Towards an Essay: My Upstate New York Journals." In *The Lovely Treachery of Words*. Toronto: Oxford 1989. 135–50.
- "The Veil of Knowing." In *The Lovely Treachery of Words*. Toronto: Oxford 1989. 179–94.
Kroetsch, Robert, James Bacque, and Pierre Gravel, eds. *Creation*. Toronto: New Press 1970.
Kroetsch, Robert, and Reingard M. Nischik, eds. *Gaining Ground: European Critics on Canadian Literature*. Edmonton: NeWest 1985.
Lecker, Robert A. "Patterns of Deception in *Wacousta*." *Journal of Canadian Fiction* 19 (1977): 77–85.
- "Bordering On: Robert Kroetsch's Aesthetic." *Journal of Canadian Studies* 17, 3 (1982): 124–33.
- *Robert Kroetsch*. Boston: Twayne 1986.
Lee, Dennis. "Cadence, Country, Silence: Writing in Colonial Space." *Boundary* 2 3, 1 (1974): 151–68.
McGregor, Gaile. *The Wacousta Syndrome: Explorations in the Canadian Langscape*. Toronto: University of Toronto Press 1985.
Macherey, Pierre. *A Theory of Literary Production*. 1966. Trans. Geoffrey Wall. London: Routledge and Kegan Paul 1978.
McKenna, Isobel. "As They Really Were: Women in the Novels of Grove." *English Studies in Canada* 2, 1 (1976): 109–16.
McMullen, Lorraine. "Women in Grove's Novels." *Inscape: The Grove Edition* (symposium issue) 11, 1 (1974): 67–76.

Malkiel, Yakov. "Changes in the European Languages under a New Set of Sociolinguistic Circumstances." In *First Images of America: The Impact of the New World on the Old*. Ed. Fredi Chiappelli, Michael J.B. Allen, and Robert L. Benson. 2 vols. Berkeley, Los Angeles, London: University of California Press 1976. 2:581–93.

Mandel, Ann. "Uninventing Structures: Cultural Criticism and the Novels of Robert Kroetsch." *Robert Kroetsch: Reflections. Open Letter* 5, 8–9 (1984): 52–6.

Meyer, Bruce, and Brian O'Riordan. "Sheila Watson. It's What You Say." *In Their Words: Interviews with Fourteen Canadian Writers*. Toronto: Anansi 1984. 157–67.

Miller, Judith. "Rummaging in the Sewing Basket of the Gods: Sheila Watson's 'Antigone.'" *Studies in Canadian Literature* 12, 2 (1987): 212–21.

Monkman, Leslie. *A Native Heritage: Images of the Indian in English-Canadian Literature*. Toronto, Buffalo, London: University of Toronto Press 1981.

Moss, John. *Sex and Violence in the Canadian Novel: The Ancestral Present*. Toronto: McClelland and Stewart 1977.

Neuman, Shirley. "Sheila Watson." In *Profiles in Canadian Literature*. Vol. 4. Ed. Jeffrey M. Heath. Toronto and Charlottetown: Dundurn Press 1982. 45–52.

Neuman, Shirley, and Robert Wilson. *Labyrinths of Voice: Conversations with Robert Kroetsch*. Edmonton: NeWest 1982.

O'Gorman, Edmundo. *The Invention of America: An Inquiry into the Historical Nature of the New World and the Meaning of Its History*. Bloomington: University of Indiana Press 1961.

Pacey, Desmond. *Frederick Philip Grove*. Toronto: Ryerson 1945.

– ed. *The Letters of Frederick Philip Grove*. Toronto and Buffalo: University of Toronto Press 1976.

Pache, Walter. "'The Fiction Makes Us Real': Aspects of Postmodernism in Canada." In *Gaining Ground: European Critics on Canadian Literature*. Ed. Robert Kroetsch and Reingard M. Nischik. Edmonton: NeWest 1985. 64–78.

– "Frederick Philip Grove; Comparative Perspectives." In *A Stranger to My Time*. Ed. Paul Hjartarson. Edmonton: NeWest 1986. 11–20.

Padolsky, Enoch. "Ethnic Voice." *Canadian Ethnic Studies* 18, 1 (1986): 109–18.

– "Grove's 'Nationhood' and the European Immigrant." *Journal of Canadian Studies* 22, 1 (1987): 32–50.

Parameswaran, Uma. "Amid the Alien Corn: Biculturalism and the Challenge of Commonwealth Literary Criticism." *World Literature Written in English* 21, 2 (1982): 240–54.

Partridge, Colin. *The Making of New Cultures: A Literary Perspective.* Amsterdam: Rodopi 1982.

Potvin, Elizabeth. "'The Eternal Feminine' and the Clothing Motif in Grove's Fiction." *Studies in Canadian Literature* 12, 2 (1987): 222–38.

Promis, Juan. *The Identity of Hispanoamerica: An Interpretation of Colonial Literature.* Trans. Alita Kelley and Alec E. Kelley. Tucson: University of Arizona Press 1991.

Renan, Ernest. "What is a Nation?" Trans. Martin Thom. In *Nation and Narration.* Ed. Homi Bhabha. London and New York: Routledge 1990. 8–22.

Richards, David. "Nineteenth-Century Scottish and Canadian Fiction: The Examples of Sir Walter Scott and Major John Richardson." In *Re-visions of Canadian Literature.* Ed. Shirley Chew. Leeds: University of Leeds 1984.

Richardson, John. *Tecumseh; or, The Warrior of the West. A Poem in Four Cantos, with Notes.* London 1828. Rpr Ottawa: Golden Dog Press 1978.

– *Ecarté; or, The Salons of Paris.* 3 vols. London 1829. Rpr 2 vols. Philadelphia: Tower and Hogan 1829.

– *Frascati's; or, Scenes in Paris.* 2 vols. London 1830. Rpr Philadelphia: E.L. Carey and A. Hart 1836.

– *Wacousta; or, The Prophecy: A Tale of the Canadas.* 1832. Rpr ed. Douglas Cronk. Ottawa: Carleton University Press 1987.

– *The Canadian Brothers; or, The Prophecy Fulfilled: A Tale of the Late American War.* 1840. Rpr intro. Carl F. Klinck. Toronto and Buffalo: University of Toronto Press 1976.

– *The Monk Knight of St. John: A Tale of the Crusades.* New York: Dewitt and Davenport 1850.

– *Westbrook, the Outlaw! or, The Avenging Wolf. An American Border Tale.* 1851. Rpr Montreal: Grant Woolmer 1973.

Riedel, Walter E., ed. *The Old World and the New.* Toronto: University of Toronto Press 1984.

Riley, Anthony W. "The Case of Greve/Grove: The European Roots of a Canadian Writer." In *The Old World and the New.* Ed. Walter E. Riedel. Toronto: University of Toronto Press 1984. 37–58.

Robertson, R.T. *The Commonwealth Writer Overseas: Themes of Exile and Expatriation.* Ed. A. Niven. Brussels: Didier 1976. 75–85.

Rooke, Constance. "Women of *The Double Hook*." In *Fear of the Open Heart: Essays on Contemporary Canadian Writing*. Toronto: Coach House 1989. 82–92.

Ross, Malcolm. Introduction to Frederick Philip Grove, *Over Prairie Trails*. 1922. Rpr Toronto: McClelland and Stewart 1970.

Ruland, Richard. *The Rediscovery of America*. Cambridge: Harvard University Press 1967.

Said, Edward. *Orientalism*. New York: Pantheon 1978.

Schafer, Jurgen. "A Farewell to Europe: Rudy Wiebe's *The Temptations of Big Bear* and Robert Kroetsch's *Gone Indian*." In *Gaining Ground: European Critics on Canadian Literature*. Ed. Robert Kroetsch and Reingard M. Nischik. Edmonton: NeWest 1985. 79–90.

Scobie, Stephen. *Sheila Watson and Her Works*. Toronto: ECW 1984.

– *Signature Event Cantext*. Edmonton: NeWest 1989.

Slavin, Arthur J. "The American Principle from More to Locke." In *First Images of America: The Impact of the New World on the Old*. Ed. Fred Chiapelli, Michael J.B. Allen, and Robert L. Benson. 2 vols. Berkeley: University of California Press 1976. 1:139–64.

Slemon, Stephen. "Monuments of Empire: Allegory/Counter-Discourse/Post-Colonial Writing." *Kunapipi* 9, 3 (1987): 1–15.

– "Magic Realism as Post-Colonial Discourse." *Canadian Literature* 116 (1988): 9–24.

– "Post-Colonial Allegory and the Transformation of History." *Journal of Commonwealth Literature* 23, 1 (1988): 157–67.

– "Unsettling the Empire: Resistance Theory for the Second World." *World Literature Written in English* 30, 2 (1990): 30–41.

Snead, James. "European Pedigrees/African Contagions: Nationality, Narrative, and Communality in Tutuola, Achebe, and Reed." In *Nation and Narration*. Ed. Homi Bhabha. London and New York: Routledge 1990: 231–49.

Spettigue, Douglas O. *Frederick Philip Grove*. Toronto: Copp Clark 1969.

– *FPG: The European Years*. Ottawa: Oberon Press 1973.

– "Fanny Essler and the Master." In *A Stranger to My Time*. Ed. Paul Hjartarson. Edmonton: NeWest 1986. 47–64.

– "Felix, Elsa, André Gide and Others: Some Unpublished Letters of F.P. Greve." *Canadian Literature* 134 (Autumn 1992): 9–39.

Spivak, Gayatri Chakravorty. "The Rani of Sirmur." In *Europe and Its Others*. Ed. Francis Barker et al. Colchester: University of Essex 1985. 128–51.

– *In Other Worlds: Essays in Cultural Politics*. New York and London: Methuen 1987.

– *The Post-Colonial Critic: Interviews, Strategies, Dialogues.* Ed. Sarah Harasym. New York and London: Routledge 1990.

Thomas, Peter. *Robert Kroetsch.* Vancouver: Douglas and McIntyre 1980.

Tiffin, Helen. "Commonwealth Literature and Comparative Methodology." *World Literature Written in English* 23, 1 (1984): 26–30.

– "Post-Colonial Literatures and Counter-Discourse." *Kunapipi* 9, 3 (1987): 17–34.

– "Recuperative Strategies in the Post-Colonial Novel." *Span* 24 (1987): 27–45.

– "Post-Colonialism, Post-Modernism and the Rehabilitation of Post-Colonial History." *Journal of Commonwealth Literature* 23, 1 (1988): 169–81.

Todorov, Tzvetan. *The Conquest of America: The Question of the Other.* 1982. Trans. Richard Howard. New York: Harper and Row 1985.

Turner, Margaret E. "The Woman in the Text: Autobiography, Intertextuality, and the Reading of Julia Cruikshank." *The Gender Issue.* ECW 54 (1994): 101–23.

Urquhart, Jane. *The Whirlpool.* Toronto: McClelland and Stewart 1986.

Watson, Sheila. *The Double Hook.* 1959. Rpr Toronto: McClelland and Stewart 1969.

– "And the Four Animals." *Five Stories.* Toronto: Coach House 1984. 73–6.

– *Five Stories.* Toronto: Coach House 1984.

– *Deep Hollow Creek.* Toronto: McClelland and Stewart 1992.

White, Hayden. *Metahistory: The Historical Imagination in Nineteenth-Century Europe.* Baltimore and London: Johns Hopkins 1973.

– "The Noble Savage Theme as Fetish." In *First Images of America: The Impact of the New World on the Old.* Ed. Fredi Chiappelli, Michael J.B. Allen, and Robert L. Benson. 2 vols. Berkeley, Los Angeles, London: University of California Press 1976. 1:121–35.

– "The Historical Text as Literary Artifact." In *The Writing of History: Literary Form and Historical Understanding.* Ed. Robert H. Canary and Henry Kozicki. Madison, Wisc.: University of Wisconsin Press 1978. 41–62.

– *Tropics of Discourse: Essays in Cultural Criticism.* Baltimore: Johns Hopkins 1978.

Wiebe, Rudy. *Playing Dead: A Contemplation Concerning the Arctic.* Edmonton: NeWest 1989.

Index